NEGOTIABLE INSTRUMENTS AND BANKING LAW AND PRACTICE

FOR BEGINNERS

SHIV NATH JHA

Made with ♥ on the Notion Press Platform
www.notionpress.com

Contents

Preface v

1. Reserve Bank Of India 1
2. Important Functions Of Reserve Bank Of India 4
3. Powers Of Reserve Bank Of India 6
4. Role Of Monetary Policy Committee 9
5. Expansionary Monetary Policy Vs Contractionary Monetary Policy 12
6. Monetary Policy Vs Fiscal Policy 14
7. Relationship Between Banker And Customer 15
8. Definition Of "banking" Under Indian Law 18
9. Principles Of Banking 20
10. Definition Of The Word "customer" 22
11. Banker-customer Relationship 24
12. Rights Of Banker 28
13. Duties Of Banker 31
14. Types Of Customers In Bank 35
15. Negotiable Instruments Act, 1881 49
16. Objectives Of Negotiable Instruments Act 52
17. Introduction 53
18. Meaning & Characteristics Of Negotiable Instruments 54
19. Presumptions As To Negotiable Instrument 56
20. Types Of Negotiable Instrument 58
21. Parties To Negotiable Instruments 67
22. Negotiation 69
23. Assignment 70
24. Endorsement 72
25. Instruments Without Consideration 77
26. Holder In Due Course 82

Contents

27. Dishonour Of A Negotiable Instrument 86

28. Noting And Protesting 90

29. Summary 93

Preface

It would be impossible within the narrow confines of one volume to deal exhaustively with so extensive a subject as that of Indian banking practice, but it is hoped that the parts of this subject dealt with herein will be found to be treated with due regard to their relative importance, and that no really essential information has been overlooked.

Furthermore, beginners could refer to this book as a study guide because this book contains concise information, and all facts, explaining the Law and Practices followed by the Banks in India.

The reader should have no difficulty in understanding the forms and methods explained in the text, and in interpreting them by his own experience. Too specific explanations have been avoided as far as possible.

Shiv Nath Jha

CHAPTER ONE

Reserve Bank of India

The Reserve Bank of India (RBI) is the central bank of India, which began operations on 1st April 1935, under the Reserve Bank of India Act. The Reserve Bank of India uses **monetary policy** to create financial stability in India, and it is charged with regulating the country's currency and credit systems.

Understanding the Reserve Bank of India (RBI)

Located in Mumbai, the RBI serves the financial market in many ways. The bank sets the overnight interbank lending rate. The Mumbai Interbank Offer Rate (MIBOR) serves as a benchmark for interest rate–related financial instruments in India.

The main purpose of the RBI is to conduct consolidated supervision of the financial sector in India, which is made up of commercial banks, financial institutions, and non-banking finance firms. Initiatives adopted by the RBI include restructuring bank inspections, introducing off-site surveillance of banks and financial institutions, and strengthening the role of auditors.

First and foremost, the RBI formulates, implements, and monitors India's monetary policy. The bank's management objective is to maintain price stability and ensure that credit is flowing to productive economic sectors. The RBI also manages all foreign exchange under the Foreign Exchange Management Act of 1999. This act allows the RBI to facilitate external trade and payments to promote the development and health of the foreign exchange market in India.

The RBI acts as a regulator and supervisor of the overall financial system. This injects public confidence into the national financial system, protects interest rates, and provides positive banking alternatives to the public. Finally, the RBI acts as the issuer of national currency. For India, this means that currency is either issued or destroyed depending on its fit for current circulation. This provides the Indian public with a supply of currency in the form of dependable notes and coins, a lingering issue in India.

Special Considerations

The RBI was originally set up as a private entity, but it was nationalized in 1949. The reserve bank is governed by a central board of directors appointed by the national government. The government has always appointed the RBI's directors, and this has been the case since the bank became fully owned by the government of India as outlined by the Reserve Bank of India Act. Directors are appointed for a period of four years.

According to its website, the current focus of the RBI is to continue its increased supervision of financial institutions, while dealing with legal issues related to bank fraud and consolidated accounting and attempting to create a supervisory rating model for its banks.

The Governor of the Reserve Bank is the Chairman of the **Board for Financial Supervision (BFS)** while the Deputy Governor in- charge of supervision is the Vice-chairman. The other two Deputy Governors of the Bank, together with four non-official directors from the Central Board of the Bank, are the members of the BFS.

Interesting Facts and Functions of RBI (Reserve Bank of India)

The central bank of India, RBI is also regarded as a bank of banks owing to the functions of RBI. It was established on April 1, 1935, under the Reserve Bank of India Act, 1934. In the beginning, the headquarters of RBI was established in Calcutta. However, soon after, in 1937, it was permanently shifted to Mumbai.

As of October 2021, the Governor of the Reserve Bank of India is Mr Shaktikanta Das. He is the 25th RBI Governor and all the RBI functions are supervised by him.

Interesting Facts about Reserve Bank of India (RBI)

The first Governor of RBI was Osborne Smith, and the first Indian governor of RBI was C D Deshmukh.

Originally, the Reserve Bank of India was privately owned; and was established as a private bank with two extra functions: the regulation and control of all banks in India, and to be the banker to the then government.

Since its nationalization in 1949, RBI has been wholly owned by the Government of India and thus, some new roles were added to the list of functions of RBI.

CHAPTER TWO

Important Functions of Reserve Bank of India

Being a central bank of India, RBI serves a critical role in regulating the financial transactions in the country. Some of the important functions of RBI are listed below:

1. Issue of Bank Notes
2. Banker to the Government
3. Custodian of the Cash Reserves of Commercial Banks
4. Custodian of country's forex reserves
5. Lender of last resort
6. Controller of credit

1. **The Issuer of Bank Notes:** The most important function of RBI is the issuance of currency notes and coins, except the one rupee note and coin which are issued by the Ministry of Finance. All other notes bear the signature of the RBI Governor. However, the agency of distribution of all notes and coins issued by the Government of India is the Reserve Bank of India.
2. **Banker to the Government:** Another chief function of RBI is that it takes care of the banking needs of the government, which includes maintaining & operating the deposit accounts of the government,

collecting the receipts of funds and making payments on behalf of the Government of India. It also represents the Indian Government, as a member of the International Monetary Fund and the World Bank.

3. **Custodian of Cash Reserves of Commercial Banks:** Commercial banks are required to maintain the cash reserves at a rate decided by the RBI in its monetary policy.
4. **Custodian of Foreign Exchange Reserve:** Another of the important functions of RBI is maintaining a reserve of foreign currencies that enables the RBI to deal with any crisis situation.
5. **Lender of the Last Resort:** As the banker of banks, the RBI acts as a parent to all commercial banks in India. Thus, it becomes the lender of the last resort for all banks when they are in a crisis situation. RBI helps them by lending money, although at higher ROI, to sail through the tide of financial difficulties.
6. **Controller of Credit:** RBI controls the credit created by the commercial banks in India, in accordance with the economic priorities of the government of India. RBI uses quantitative and qualitative methods to control and regulate the flow of money in the market. These are implemented by announcing monetary policies at regular intervals. The monetary policy involves the management of interest rates and money supply. The central bank of India tweaks the money supply to achieve objectives such as liquidity, inflation, and consumption.

CHAPTER THREE

POWERS OF RESERVE BANK OF INDIA

Under Banking Regulation Act the RBI enjoys the following powers:

Section 10 BB – Power of Reserve Bank to appoint Chairman of the Board of Directors appointed on a whole-time basis or a Managing Director of a banking company.

Where the office of the Chairman of the Board of Directors appointed on a whole-time basis or a Managing Director of a banking company is vacant, the Reserve Bank may, if in its opinion that the continuation of such vacancy is likely to adversely affect the interests of the banking company, appoint a person as Chairman of the Board of Directors or a Managing Director of the banking company.

Section 21 – Power of Reserve Bank to control advances by banking companies: Reserve Bank has the powers to determine policies and direct banking companies to follow the same.

Section 22 – Licensing of banking companies: All Banking companies need to get a licence from RBI and it issues licence only after 'tests of entry' are fulfilled.

Section 24A Power to exempt a Co-operative bank: Without prejudice to the provisions of section 53, the RBI by notification in the Official Gazette, declare that, the whole or any part of the provisions of section 18 or section 24, as may be specified therein, shall not apply to any co-operative bank.

Section 27 – Monthly returns and power to call for other returns and information: At any time, the RBI may direct a banking company to furnish it with such statements and information relating to the business or affairs of the banking company (including any business or affairs with which such banking company is concerned) as RBI may consider necessary or expedient to obtain for the purposes of this Act, apart from calling for information every half-year regarding the investments of a banking company and the classification of its advances in respect of industry, commerce and agriculture.

Section 29A – Power in respect of associate enterprises: The RBI may direct a banking company to annex to its financial statements or furnish to it separately, within such time or intervals, necessary statements and information relating to the business or affairs of any associate enterprise of the banking company. It can also conduct an inspection of any associate enterprise of a banking company and its books of account jointly by one or more of its officers or employees or other persons along with the Board or authority regulating such associate enterprise.

Section 30 – Power to order Special audit: In the public interest or in the interest of the banking company or its depositors, the RBI may at any time by order direct that a special audit of the banking company's accounts.

Section 35 – Inspection of Banking Companies: Reserve Bank on its own or being directed so to do by the Central Government, inspect any banking company and its books and accounts and supply to the banking company a copy of its report on such inspection.

Section 35A – Power of the Reserve Bank to give directions: In the public interest or in the interest of Banking policy RBI has powers to issue, modify or cancel as it deems fit, and the banking companies or the banking company, are bound to comply with such directions.

Section 36 – Further powers and functions of Reserve Bank: RBI may caution or prohibit banking companies or any banking company in particular against entering into any particular transaction or class of transactions.

- On a request by the companies concerned and subject to the provision of section 44A, assist, in the amalgamation of such banking companies.
- Give assistance to any banking company by means of a loan or advance in terms of under section 18 of the RBI Act.
- Direct the banking company to

- Call for a meeting of Directors or
- Discuss such matters with Officers of RBI,
- Depute an officer to such meeting, appoint observers to such meetings

- Furnish information of such meetings
- Make changes in management.

In addition to the above the RBI has also been vested with powers to remove managerial and other persons from office (section 36AA), to appoint additional Directors (section 36AB), to issue directions in respect of stressed assets (Section 35AB), Supersede Board of Directors in certain cases (Section 36ACA), Supersede Board of Directors of a multi-State Co-operative bank (Section 36AAA) and also to impose penalty (Section 47).

In addition to the above, RBI also enjoys certain powers vis-a-vis banks under RBI Act as per the following table

SNO	Power	Section
1	Power of direct discount.	18
2	Power to require returns from co-operative banks.	44
3	Power to collect credit information.	45B
4	Power to call for returns containing credit information	45C
5	Power to determine policy and issue directions	45JA
6	Power to call for information from financial institutions and to give directions.	45L
7	Power to regulate transactions in derivatives (excluding capital market derivatives), money market instruments	45W
8	Power of Bank to depute its employees to other institutions	54AA
9	Power of the (RBI's) Central Board to make regulations	58

CHAPTER FOUR

ROLE OF MONETARY POLICY COMMITTEE

The Reserve Bank of India Act, 1934 (RBI Act) was amended by the Finance Act, 2016, to provide for a statutory and institutionalized framework for a Monetary Policy Committee, for maintaining price stability, while keeping in mind the objective of growth. The Monetary Policy Committee is entrusted with the task of fixing the benchmark policy rate (repo rate) required to contain inflation within the specified target level.

What are the instruments of monetary policy?

Some of the following instruments are used by RBI as a part of their monetary policies.

Open Market Operations: An open market operation is an instrument which involves buying/selling of securities like government bond from or to the public and banks. The RBI sells government securities to control the flow of credit and buys government securities to increase credit flow.

Cash Reserve Ratio (CRR): Cash Reserve Ratio is a specified amount of bank deposits which banks are required to keep with the RBI in the form of reserves or balances. The higher the CRR with the RBI, the lower will be the liquidity in the system and vice versa. The CRR was reduced from 15% in 1990 to 5 % in 2002.

Statutory Liquidity Ratio (SLR): All financial institutions have to maintain a certain quantity of liquid assets with themselves at any point in time of their total time and demand liabilities. This is known as the Statutory Liquidity Ratio. The assets are kept in non-cash forms such as precious metals, bonds, etc.

Bank Rate Policy: Also known as the discount rate, bank rates are interest charged by the RBI for providing funds and loans to the banking system. An increase in bank rate increases the cost of borrowing by commercial banks which results in the reduction in credit volume to the banks and hence the supply of money declines.

An increase in the bank rate is the symbol of the tightening of the RBI monetary policy.

Credit Ceiling: With this instrument, RBI issues prior information or direction that loans to the commercial bank will be given up to a certain limit. In this case, a commercial bank will be tight in advancing loans to the public. They will allocate loans to limited sectors.

A few examples of credit ceiling are agriculture sector advances and priority sector lending.

Monetary Policy Tools

Federal funds rate. Commonly called the fed funds rate, or the fed funds target rate, this is the target interest rate set by the Federal Open Market Committee (FOMC) at its eight yearly meetings. Commercial banks reference the fed funds rate when they lend their excess reserves to each other overnight.

Open market operations

The Fed buys and sells government securities, like Treasury bills and bonds, in the open market. By buying back securities, the Fed effectively increases the supply of money circulating—conversely, selling securities lowers the supply.

Historically, open market operations are the most commonly used tool to conduct monetary policy.

Reserve requirements

The Fed keeps a close eye on reserve requirements, or the amount of cash banks must have on hand at any time to comply with banking regulations. Those reserves must either be secured in bank vaults or via a deposit in a qualified Federal Reserve Bank to ensure they have money available should customers need it. By lowering the amount of cash banks are required to keep on hand, the Fed can encourage banks to lend out more money. And by raising that requirement, it can do the inverse.

The Discount rate

This is the interest rate charged by the Fed on short-term loans to financial institutions. Generally, these loans are meant to cover reserve requirements or liquidity issues banks can't meet through loans from other banks, which offer a lower federal funds borrowing rate. Typically, when the U.S. economy is humming on all cylinders, discount rates are relatively high because the Fed doesn't need to make borrowing money cheap to incentivize activity.

However, when the economy is in a slump, the Fed often lowers interest rates to spur lending and credit to individuals and businesses.

Quantitative easing (QE)

With QE, a central bank like the Federal Reserve uses its massive cash reserves to buy up large-scale financial assets like government and corporate bonds as well as stocks. This may sound similar to open markets, but quantitative easing often takes place on a much larger scale in more dire circumstances, involves buying more than just shorter-term government bonds and generally occurs when interest rates are already at or near 0%, meaning the Fed has already fully extended one of its primary weapons. Central banks must be careful with QE, however, because continued large-scale asset purchases can lead to economic conditions monetary policy makers don't want, like higher inflation and asset bubbles.

Public service announcements

When implementing a nation's monetary policy, a central bank will announce to the financial markets and the general public its general outlook on the economy and any policy measures its taking. In and of themselves, these PSAs may influence the market and economy in ways that the central bank is hoping for.

CHAPTER FIVE

Expansionary Monetary Policy vs Contractionary Monetary Policy

Depending on the economic circumstance, monetary policy may be categorized in one of two ways: expansionary monetary policy or contractionary monetary policy.

Expansionary Monetary Policy

Also known as loose monetary policy, expansionary policy increases the supply of money and credit to generate economic growth. A central bank may deploy an expansionist monetary policy to reduce unemployment and boost growth during hard economic times.

It usually does so by lowering its benchmark federal funds rate, or the interest rate banks use when they lend each other money to satisfy any reserve requirements. While in the U.S. the Federal Reserve cannot require a certain federal funds rate, it can set guidelines and influence the rate banks charge each other by altering the supply of money. In turn, this may lower other interest rates, like those banks use when they lend money to consumers, which helps spur consumer spending through increased credit and lending throughout the nation's economy.

For example, when the U.S. banking system collapsed leading to the Great Recession of 2007-2008, the Federal Reserve cut interest rates to near-zero to jumpstart the U.S. economy, thus "expanding" economic growth. It recently did the same thing to pull the country out of the 2020

Covid-19 recession.

Contractionary Monetary Policy

Also known as tight monetary policy, contractionary policy decreases a nation's money supply to curb rampant inflation and keep the economy in balance. A central bank will likely hike interest rates and try to slow the growth of money and prices.

At the outset of the 1980s, for instance, when the U.S. inflation rate soared to almost 15%, the Fed aggressively raised interest rates to nearly 20%. While that move led to a nationwide recession, it also brought inflation back to about 3%, helping set the stage for a robust U.S. economy for the remainder of the decade.

CHAPTER SIX

Monetary Policy vs Fiscal Policy

Monetary Policy vs Fiscal Policy

When it comes to regulating the economy, a country has two main levers it can pull: monetary policy and fiscal policy.

While they might sound similar—both involve words that suggest money or finance—they're quite different and are enacted by distinct sectors of the government. Monetary policy is controlled by the Federal Reserve; fiscal policy, on the other hand, is driven by the U.S. government's executive and the legislative branches.

Practically speaking, this means "fiscal policy deals with taxation and government spending". In contrast, monetary policy involves effecting change by manipulating the monetary supply.

CHAPTER SEVEN

Relationship between Banker and Customer

OBJECTIVES:-

To know the meaning of Banker and Customer

- To understand the general relationship between banker and customer
- To understand the special relationships between banker and customer in various capacities

INTRODUCTION : The word "Bank" is derived from an Italian word "Banco" which means "a bench", on which money changers sat and did their business in ancient days.

- In 1587 - "Banco de Rialto" was first set up in Venice
- In 1609 - Bank of Amsterdam was set-up
- In 1619 - "Banco Del Giro" took over "Banco de Rialto"
- In 1694 - Bank of England was set up and became as Central Bank of the country

Indian Scenario

- In 1786 - The Indian Banking History started with establishment of "General Bank of India", followed by "Bank of Hindustan" and "Bengal Bank"

- In 1809 - Presidency Bank of Bengal was established
- In 1840 - Presidency Bank of Bombay was established
- In 1843 - Presidency Bank of Madras was established
- In 1934 - Reserve Bank of India was formed by passing RBI Act, 1934. RBI was Nationalized on 1st January, 1949 by passing Transfer of Public Ownership Act
- In March 1949- Banking companies Act was passed, which gave more powers to RBI (to control the working of Commercial Banks)
- In 1955 - The Imperial Bank of India was nationalized and came into existence as "State Bank of India". Then seven subsidiary banks, for State Bank, were set up and they together were called by the name "SBI Group"
- On 19th July 1969 - 14 major Scheduled Banks in the country were nationalized [Scheduled Commercial Bank is one which is included in the 2nd schedule of RBI, Act]
- In 1980 - Six more commercial banks were nationalized.

As on 16th Oct 2022, India is having 12 public sector Banks, 21 Private Sectors Banks functioning in our country, along with 46 foreign banks which are also operating in India now.

Indian Banking System

Indian Banking system is a Branch Banking system, regulated by the Reserve Bank of India as the apex banking authority in the country. It is patterned on British Banking system, having 'Bank of England' as the banking regulator.

Meaning of "Banker"

The words "Banker" and "Bank" are used interchangeably. The Cambridge dictionary says the word 'Bank' means "ability to pay" as opposite to the word "bankrupt" which means "inability to pay".

According to Dr. Herbert L. Heart "A banker is one who in the ordinary course of his business, honours cheques drawn upon him by persons from and for whom he receives money on current accounts".

According to Sir John Paget "No person or body corporate or otherwise can be a banker who does not,

- accept deposit account
- accept current accounts
- issue and pay cheques and

- Collect cheques crossed or uncrossed for his customers.

From these definitions, we can arrive at a common concept of banking. Accordingly a banker is one who

- accepts deposits
- Grants loans and undertakes investments.

Before understanding the complete meaning of the word "Banker", first we have to understand the meaning of the word "Banking", also.

CHAPTER EIGHT

DEFINITION OF "BANKING" UNDER INDIAN LAW

In India, 'banking' has been defined by Banking Regulation Act, 1949 (vide Sections 5b, c) as follows:-

- Accepting, for the purpose of lending (or)
- Investment of deposits of money received from the public
- Repayable on demand and
- Withdrawable by cheque, draft, order or otherwise [Section – 5(b)]

A Banking company is "a company which transacts the business of banking in India" [section 5 (c)].

From the above definitions, we can understand that the following are the core functions a bank.

- Acceptance of Deposits from the public.
- Making deposits of customers withdrawable by cheque or otherwise (Withdrawal slip, letter, voucher etc) on demand or repayable on maturity to the customers.
- Lending or investing funds collected from customer, subject to the obligation to repay the deposits to the customer on demand or otherwise as per the term of the deposits.

To execute the above functions, in a complete and excellent way, banks follow some suitable and prudent policies.

CHAPTER NINE

PRINCIPLES OF BANKING

Principle of Intermediation: Banks are called financial intermediaries, as they mediate between the depositors (savers of money) and borrowers (users of money). Banks invest or lend funds of depositors who themselves are unable to lend their funds, due to risk. Banks have expertise and abilities to manage such risks.

Principle of Liquidity: The simultaneous operations of accepting the deposits (repayable on demand or on certain maturity periods) and lending these funds to borrowers in a manner such that the bank would be able to arrange for the funds, without interruption.

Principle of Profitability: Banking business, like any other, aims at profit in order to sustain the required growth. The banks earn profit by way of interest income (interest on loans and investments and fee based income, charges of various kinds, commission etc).

Interest Income: The differential spread of interest between loans and deposits rates, is the interest Income. It is the main source of profit for a bank. The interest earned by a bank on its lending operations should be higher than the interest paid by it on its deposit operations.

Non-Interest or fee-based income: Non-Interest income is earned by banks by way of commission on issue of drafts, letters of credit, funds remittance, foreign exchange business and other ancillary services.

Principle of Solvency: Banks plough back a good portion of their profits into their business to enhance the reserves and financial strength of banks. It is also essential for compliance of the regulatory guidelines regarding Capital Adequacy Ratio, asset classification and provisioning for nonperforming assets etc. This is the principle of solvency, which also enables liquidity and profitability.

Principle of Trust: The Principle of Trust indicates the "confidence or dependability" as perceived by customers and public in relation to a bank.

The public confidence in a bank arises from the cumulative result of the policies of liquidity, profitability, and solvency and governance quality followed by each bank over a long period.

In the light of these principles we shall analyse the relationships between a "Banker" and customer.

CHAPTER TEN

DEFINITION OF THE WORD "CUSTOMER"

According to Sir John Paget "to constitute a customer, there must be some recognizable course or habit of dealing in the nature of regular banking business" So,

- A customer is one who deals with the bank
- The dealing of the customer must be in the nature of regular banking business

There is no statutory definition of the term 'Customer' in India under Banking Regulation Act, 1949 or and other relevant Act. We have to look to the judicial pronouncement for its definition. For example, the judgement pronounced in the Great Western Railway Co vs. London and County Banking co Limited, (1901 A.C414) defines a customer as follows:

- A customer is a person who has some sort of account, either deposit or current account or some similar relations with a bank. From this, it follows that any person may become a customer by opening a deposit or current account or similar relation with a bank.

The above judgement has been also followed by Indian Courts as regards the meaning or essential elements of a customer. By opening a Bank account Current, Savings, Fixed Deposit etc., in one's name and by depositing required money in such an account, a person becomes the customer of that particular branch of the bank.

Once a person becomes customer, the relationship between the Bank and Customer gets started legally and may take different forms, depending upon the type of banking services the customer is availing from the bank.

CHAPTER ELEVEN

BANKER-CUSTOMER RELATIONSHIP

The main relationship between bank and a customer is that of debtor -creditor in the case of deposit account and creditor-debtor in the case of overdraft or loan account. The bank acts trustee in case of valuables entrusted with the bank branch and as agent or bailee in other kinds of transactions. These kinds of relationships enjoin different rights and duties on the bank, involving different degrees of care and diligence as below:

The Relationship between banker and customer can be in the form of

I. Debtor - Creditor
II. Trustee - Beneficiary
III. Agent - Principal
IV. Bailor - Bailee
V. Assignor – Assignee

I) Debtor-Creditor: A debtor is an entity that owes a debt to another entity. The entity may be an individual, a firm, a government, a company or other legal person. When the counterpart of this debt arrangement is a bank, the debtor is more often referred to as a borrower.

<u>Bank as debtor</u>

The principal relationship of bank-customer is that of debtor-creditor in case of deposit accounts like Savings Bank account, Current account, Fixed Deposit account and Recurring deposit account.

<u>Bank as creditor</u>

The relationship between bank-customer becomes that of creditor-debtor, when customer has borrowed money from the bank by way of

Secured or Unsecured loans like Business Loan, Personal Loan, Housing Loan, Auto Loan, OD(Overdraft), CC(Cash credit), Demand loan, Term loan, Bills discount or any other kind of loan or advance, either on secured or unsecured basis.

The relationship between banker and customer is primarily that of a debtor-creditor and the respective position is determined by the state of the account. This means when a banker receives deposit from a customer, if the deposit is to the credit of the customer, the banker becomes a debtor and the customer creditor.

Thus, in all savings accounts where the customer's account is in credit balance, the banker is the debtor and the customer, creditor.

DIFFERENCE BETWEEN NORMAL DEBTOR-CREDITOR RELATIONSHIP AND BANKER-CUSTOMER RELATIONSHIP

Normal Debtor - Creditor	Banker – Customer
Debtor makes repayment of Debt even without demand from creditor	Only when the customer demands payment through presentation of a cheque, the Banker makes payment.
Interest rate is normally decided by the creditor	Interest is decided by the debtor, the banker
Creditor can demand repayment of loan at any time / moment.	Customer as a creditor has to demand only during the working hours of the bank.
Creditor can make oral (or) written demand.	Customer should demand in the proper manner by the presentation of cheques or withdrawal slip or any other mode as prescribed by the Bank.
According to law of limitation, the repayment should be done by the debtor within three years from the date of loan.	Here, the law of limitation commence from the date of demand made by the customer on his Deposit.

II) Trustee – Beneficiary: Trustee is an individual who is responsible for a property or an organization on behalf of some other individual or a third party. Trustee is supposed to make profitable decision for the entity under it authorization. It is a legal relationship between the trustee and the party, where the trustee is totally responsible for the maintenance, performance, and profitability of the trust under his guidance.

A beneficiary is any person who gains an advantage and/or profits from something.

This relation works out when the,

- Customer deposits money for a specific purpose, the banker is a trustee and the customer beneficiary. As such, the banker has to employ the funds for a specific purpose for which it is meant.
- Banker becomes a trustee whenever he undertakes to collect cheques on behalf of customers. After realizing, banker has to credit the proceeds to the account of the customer. When the amount is credited to the account of the customer, the relationship changes wherein the banker becomes a debtor and the customer creditor.
- Customer deposits securities and valuables for safe custody with the banker. The banker in such a case is a trustee and so, whenever the customer demands the securities, the banker has to return them to the customer who is a beneficiary.
- In the case of companies, when they receive debenture amount from the public, the banker acts as one of the trustees of the company and so has a responsibility to review the value of the assets against which the debentures are issued. Hence, the banker has a responsibility to supervise the property of the company for which he is a trustee.

III) Agent – Principal: An agent is a person who acts for or represents another. The principal is the person who gives authority to another, called an agent, to act on his or her behalf. Banker acts as an agent of a customer, when

- Purchasing and selling securities on behalf of the customers.
- Collecting dividend warrants and interest warrants
- Paying club subscription, insurance premium, rent and other bills, as per instruction of the customer

Here again, the relationship cannot be called in the true sense as agent - principal. In the case of a normal agent-principal relationship, the agent has to render accounts to the principal and should also inform the principal how the amount given to him by the principal has been spent or invested. In other words, the agent has to render accounts to the principal while dealing with the funds of the principal.

However in the case of a banker- customer relationship, though the banker is dealing with the money belonging to the customer, he need not render accounts to the customer or inform the customer as to how the money is lent or invested. Though the money invested or lent, belong to the customers,the banker need not tell them the extent of profit or return he made from such investment or loan. But in the case of normal agent-principal relationship, it is the duty of the agent to render accounts to the principal and also inform the return earned on the investment.

Thus, though a banker may act as an agent of customer, in the true legal sense, he is not an agent and so he need not render account for the money deposited with him.

IV) Bailor – Bailee: A bailor is a person who entrusts a piece of his or her property to another person (the bailee). A bailee does not have ownership of the property. When a customer borrows from a bank against the security under pledge, the bank is regarded not only a pledge but also a bailee and so the bank has to take care of the security until it is returned to the customer. But the goods kept in the safe deposit vault will not come under bailment. The customer is keeping the goods in the safe deposit vault secretly and hence the banker will not be a bailee. As a bailee, the goods coming into his custody will be protected and the banker is totally aware of the nature of the goods. Thus, the banker will act as a bailee only when goods are entrusted to him for a specific purpose. Any expenses incurred towards maintenance of the security or goods have to be borne by the customer.

V) Assignor – Assignee: An assignor is a person who transfers property rights or powers to another. An assignee is a person or entity to which property rights or powers are transferred. An assignee is the one to whom assignments are made. Whenever a bank gives loan against life insurance policy or book debts or supply bills, the banker is the assignee and the customer the assignor. Under assignment, the actionable claim of the customer is transferred to the bank as security for loan. Thus, assignment is done by customers whenever they take loan against insurance policy or book debts. Even contractors after undertaking public works for the government, obtain loan from the bank by assigning the supply bills in favour of the bank.

CHAPTER TWELVE

RIGHTS OF BANKER

1) Right of set-off : A debtor can recover any debt due from a creditor before settlement of debt with the creditor. This is called "Right of set-off"

When a bank accepts deposit from customer, he is a Debtor

When a bank lends money to the customer, the banker is a creditor and customer becomes Debtor.

In this situation, if the customer approaches the bank for closing his deposit account, the bank will allow the customer to close the account only after recovering the loan taken by the customer, from his deposit money.

Three conditions are to be fulfilled to exercise right of set-off

- The same customer should have the deposit account and loan account
- The loan must be outstanding and overdue when the loan amount is not overdue, the right of set-off cannot be exercised.
- There should not be any agreement between the banker and customer, by which the banker is prevented from exercising right of set-off.

Right of set-off can be exercised when a partner's individual account has a credit balance and the firm's account has a debit balance, due to loan taken from bank. But vice-versa cannot be done.

2) Right of Lien : Lien is a right of a banker, by which he can retain any security coming to his possession for the purpose of any loan due by customer.

Banker's right of general lien

One of the important rights enjoyed by a banker is the right of general lien. Lien means the right of the creditor to retain goods and securities owned by the debtor until the debt due from him is paid. It may either be general or particular. Bankers most undoubtedly have a general lien on all securities deposited with them as bankers unless there is an express or implied contract inconsistent with lien. In India sec 171 of the Indian Contract Act confers general lien upon bankers as follows - Bankers may in absence of a contract to the contrary, retain as security for a general balance of account, any goods bailed to them.

Circumstances for exercising general lien

1) No agreement inconsistent with the right of lien.

2) Property must be possessed in his capacity as a banker.

3) Possession should be lawfully obtained.

4) Property should not be entrusted to the banker for a specific purpose.

Incidents of lien- lien attaches to

1) Bills of exchange or cheques deposited for collection or pending discount.

2) Dividend warrants and interest warrants paid to the banker under mandates issued by the customer.

3) Securities deposited to secure specific loan but left in banker's hand after loan is repaid.

4) Securities, negotiable or not, which the banker has purchased or taken up, at the request of customer, for the amount paid.

Exceptions- banker has no general lien

1) On safe custody deposits.

2) On securities or bills of exchange entrusted for specific purpose.

3) On articles left by mistake or negligence.

4) On deposit account.

5) On stolen bond.

6) Until due date of the loan.

7) On trust account.

8) On title deeds of immovable properties.

3) Right of appropriation : This is a right exercised by a creditor upon his debtor for the purpose of setting loan account. Sec. 59 to 61 of the Indian contract Act deal with the provisions of the right of appropriation of payments.

In right of appropriation, we find how a debtor who has three or four debit account settler by making payments to the credits.

Condition Applying:

1. When making payment to a creditors debtor has right to inform the creditor, that as towards which loan he is making. (Section 59).

2. When a debtor has not exercised his right, the creditor has the right to appropriate the payment made by debtor towards any loan, according to his discrete (section. 60).
3. When neither the debtor nor the creditor exercises their right for appropriation, then it is the chronological order in which the debit entries have arisen, the credit entries will go to discharge the debit entries.

4) Right to charge, interest, commission and brokerage : A banker grants loan and advances to customers and charges interest on the same banker usually debit the customer's account when the customer fails to pay the interest amount every month. After three months the interest will be added to the principal amount. Interest will be then charged on the new principal amount.

- Similarly for collecting cheques, dividends and interest warrants, the banker can commission and brokerage charges.

5) Right to close the account of undesirable customer : Un-desirable customer is one who has been frequently issuing cheques which are bouncing or which are getting dishonored. Due to this, the reputation of the banker is affected. In such situation, the banker, after giving due notices to the customer can close the account.

CHAPTER THIRTEEN

DUTIES OF BANKER

1) Duty to honour cheque

It is the duty of the banker to honour cheque of customer which are drawn properly and presented during the working hours of the bank. However the Bank has the right to dishonour the cheques under the following situations.

Date

- Post dated - a date yet to come
- Stale - more than 3 months

Post dated cheques are those which carry a date which is yet to come. If a banker honours a post dated cheque, he will not only lose statutory protection but will be sued by the customer.

In the case of a stale cheque, when the cheque is more than three months old, it is no more a cheque.

Payee

- Not clear
- Wrong person

When the payee is not clear or when the payee is a wrong person, the banker will not pay and has every right to dishonour.

Amount - In words and figures differ.

When the amount given in words and stated in figure differs, the banker will dishonour.

Signature - If the signature is not according to the specimen signature or differs from the specimen, the banker should dishonour.

Endorsements - The endorsements appearing on the cheque should be proper and if there is any defect in endorsements, the cheque will be dishonoured.

Insufficient funds - If there are insufficient funds in the account and the cheque presented is for a higher amount, the bank will dishonour the cheque and mention the reason as "insufficient funds".

Mutilated Cheque - Where the cheques are torn and are beyond recognition.

Smudged Cheque - Where the writing on cheque is unclear or smudged because of sweat or water, the banker will dishonour such cheques.

Material Alteration - When a cheque contains alterations which are made without the knowledge of the drawer or the banker, with an intention to defraud both parties, the cheque will be dishonoured.

If overwriting or cancellation which are not approved by the drawer, with his full signature on the cheque, at the place of overwriting. The cheque will be dishonoured. As per latest CTS guidelines only date alteration is allowed on cheques.

2) Duty to Maintain Secrecy of Customer's Account

The banker has an obligation towards customer to maintain secrecy about the status of account. He should not reveal the secrecy of customer's account in the normal course of business. However, in the following conditions the secrecy of the customer's account will be disclosed.

- Express or Implied condition
- Under compulsion of law
- In the course of banking business
- Disclosure in the public interest
- Bankers among themselves.

I) Express or implied condition

- When customer has given in writing to the banker to reveal the secrecy of customer, the banker may do so. This is Expressed condition.
- When the customer acts as a guarantor for a principal Debtor, the banker has to reveal the secrecy of the customer's account to the guarantor. It is implied condition.

II) Under Compulsion of Law

- Under Income Tax Act 1961, when the Income-Tax authorities demand for the details of the customer's account, the banker has to reveal.

- Under Foreign Exchange Regulation Act.
- Under Indian Penal Code, when any police official makes an enquiry.
- Under Gift Tax Act.
- Under RBI Act.
- Enquiries by Government, both State and Central.
- Under Banking Companies Act, the Central Government and Reserve Bank of India can ask the banker about status of any account.
- Under Indian companies Act sec. 235, 237 and 251.
- Under Section 4 of Banker's Book Evidence Act. A banker can produce for any investigation, the books, and documents belonging to the customer.

III) In the course of Banking Business

A bank, in order to protect its own interest, may have to reveal the secrecy of the customer's account.

The banker may disclose the state of his customer's account in order to legally protect his own interest. For, example- if the banker has to recover the dues from the customer or the guarantor, disclosure of necessary facts to the guarantor or the solicitor becomes necessary and is justified.

IV) Disclosure in the Public Interest

When a customer is amassing wealth by cheating the public and increasing the deposit account with the banker it is the duty of the bank to reveal the same to the public. Otherwise the banker will be held liable for abetting the crime.

V) Bankers among themselves can share information

Between the bankers as per the trade custom, information can be shared in their own business interests. This is as per the custom of the trade.

It is an established banking practice to provide credit information about their customers by one bank to another. The customer gives implied consent to this practice at the time of opening the account.

3) Duty to render proper account of deposits made and withdrawn by customer.

It is the duty of the banker to render proper account of deposits and withdrawals by the customer by making entries in passbook and statement of account of customers.

It is the duty of the customer to verify the entries in the pass book then and there and inform the banker about the discrepancies, if any, shown in the pass book.

CHAPTER FOURTEEN

TYPES OF CUSTOMERS IN BANK

Bank is an important service sector organization. Customers play the most significant part in bank. Customer is the one who uses the banking products and services and judges the quality of those products and services. Banking relationship is a contract between the Bank & the Customer.

Types of Customers

During the opening of accounts, the banker deals with different types of customers. The banker should acquaint himself with various laws governing different types of customers. The customers can be classified as follows:

1. Personal accounts

Banker should take care and verify the certain fact while opening of accounts of individual. As per Indian Contract Act 1872, a person is competent to enter into a valid contract and open a bank account provided:

- Individual should be major, i.e. of 18 years of age;
- He should be sound mind;
- He is otherwise not disqualified by any law;
- He Should not be an insolvent;
- Drunken person is not legally competent to enter into a contract;
- He should be in good sense while lending a loan and entering into a contract.

Various types of personal accounts in banks are as under:

a) Accounts of Single Individual: This is purely a personal account in the name of an individual and is normally operated upon by the account holder himself. The account holder may authorise another person to operate on his account. For this purpose, he gives a Mandate or executes a Power of Attorney in favour of such a person.

In order to avoid legal complications that may arise after the death of the account holder, it is desirable to suggest opening of a joint account in the names of two individuals (unless it is essential in certain circumstances to open an account in the single name only), and/or to obtain proper nomination.

b) Joint Accounts of Individuals: A joint account is opened in the names of more than one individual for convenience of operations and/ or to avoid legal complications upon death of one of the joint account holders. A joint account is neither a partnership nor a trust account. It is important to obtain clear and unambiguous instructions regarding the mode of operation and repayment of balance of a joint account in the event of death of one or more joint account holder(s). Different types of operational instructions are as under:

i. Jointly or Survivor
ii. Either or Survivor
iii. Former or Survivor
iv. any one or Survivor

One or more of the joint account holders can authorize operation on the account on his/their behalf by giving a Mandate or executing a Power of Attorney, but, such Mandate or Power of Attorney must be given by all the parties to the accounts. Addition/deletion of any name, material alteration, closure of account & operational instructions in the joint account can be changed by all the account holders jointly. However, in joint accounts with operational instructions "Former or Survivor", instructions can be changed / revoked only by Former.

c) Illiterate person: Illiterate person is a person who cannot read or write. Such persons are competent to enter in to a valid contract. The account (other than Current Account) of such a person may be opened provided he calls on the Bank with a latest passport size photograph. Photograph is essential for identification. Thereupon, his thumb impression or mark should be obtained on the account opening form/card in the presence of the Bank's official. Such thumb impressions or marks affixed by illiterate persons on instruments are equivalent to their signatures. Any withdrawal/repayment of deposit amount and/or interest by way of withdrawal form or otherwise should similarly be affixed with the thumb impression or mark of the depositor.

d) Blind Persons: Blind Persons can operate the account in bank. Signature of Thumb impression of blind person in the A/c opening form to be witnessed by a person who should certify that contents of the A/c opening form were explained to the blind person in his presence. The sign may be authorized by bank officer and a witness known to both the bank and the blind person. He should always visit the branch for cash withdrawal. As per all banking facilities including net banking, ATM, Cheque Book, Locker facility, loans to be offered to visually challenged customers without discrimination.

e) Minors' Accounts: A minor is a person below the age of 18 years. A minor is under legal incapacity to contract by himself and, therefore, a guardian recognized by law along can deal with the person and property of the minor. The term "guardian" includes a natural guardian or guardian appointed by the Court of Law. Ordinarily, an account of a minor is opened and operated upon by the natural guardian of the minor or by the guardian appointed by the Court.

According to **RBI guidelines (RBI/2013-14/581DBOD. No. Leg. BC. 108/09.07.005/ 2013-14)** with a view to promote the objective of financial inclusion and also to bring uniformity among banks in opening and operating minors' accounts, banks are advised as under:

- A savings /fixed / recurring bank deposit account can be opened by a minor of any age through his/her natural or legally appointed guardian.

- Minors above the age of 10 years may be allowed to open and operate savings bank accounts independently, if they so desire. Banks may, however, keeping in view their risk management systems, fix limits in terms of age and amount up to which minors may be allowed to operate the deposit accounts independently. They can also decide, in their own discretion, as to what minimum documents are required for opening of accounts by minors.

- On attaining majority, the erstwhile minor should confirm the balance in his/her account and if the account is operated by the natural guardian / legal guardian, fresh operating instructions and specimen signature of erstwhile minor should be obtained and kept on record for all operational purposes.

Banks are free to offer additional banking facilities like internet banking, ATM/ debit card, cheque book facility etc., subject to the safeguards that minor accounts are not allowed to be overdrawn and that these always remain in credit.

It is permissible to open any type of deposit account in the name of and/or to be operated upon by a minor within the framework of rules of business of the Bank as outlined hereunder, but no Current Account should be opened.

According to Section 26 of NI Act, a minor can draw, endorse or negotiate a cheque or a bill but he cannot be held liable on such cheques or bill. Minor can be admitted to the benefits of partnership with the consent of other partners but cannot be made liable for the losses. A minor may be appointed as an agent on behalf of his principal but legally he cannot be held responsible to his principal.

When the minor becomes major he has the sole right to operate the account and guardian's power ceases. The payment should be made to the erstwhile minor upon provided his identity. When the account is operated upon by the guardian on behalf of the minor a Balance Confirmation Letter duly signed by the erstwhile minor and verified by the guardian. If account is operated by the minor himself, the erstwhile minor should be asked to sign a Balance Confirmation Letter.

List of KYC documents card

Identity and Address Proof

- Passport
- Driving Licence issued by the Regional Transport Authority
- Voter ID
- OB card issued by the National Rural Employment Guarantee Act (NREGA), signed by a State Government Officer
- Letter from the National Population Register
- Proof of possession of complete Aadhaar number.
- PAN Card issued in India is no longer considered as a valid identity proof

Communication Address Proof

If the above address proof does not contain a communication address, then the following documents can be considered as a proof of address. In such cases, the customer will have to update the Officially Valid Documents (OVD) with a communication address and submit it to the Bank within 3 months of opening the account.

- Utility Bill, which is not older than 2 months (electricity, telephone, post-paid mobile phone, piped gas, water bill).
- Property Tax Bill or Municipal Tax receipt, which is not older than one year.
- Letter of Allotment for accommodation from an employer, issued by the State Government or Central Government Departments, statutory or regulatory bodies, Public Sector undertakings, Scheduled Commercial Banks, financial institutions and listed companies.
- Leave and Licence Agreement with any of the above employers. The agreement must contain the customer's name as the employee.
- Pension or family pension payment orders issued to retired employees by Government departments or Public Sector undertakings, if they contain the address.

2. Hindu Undivided Family (HUF)

Hindu Undivided Family' otherwise known as 'Joint Hindu Family' property, business or ancestral estates and its common possession, enjoyment ownership is the basis of formation of HUF.As per Hindu law, the Hindus, Sikhs, & Jains can form HUF. HUF is governed basically by two schools of thought. In Bengal, it is governed by Dayabhag Law. In other parts of India, it is governed by Mitakshara Law. The law governing Hindu Undivided Family is codified under Hindu Code and now, succession among Hindu is governed by Hindu Succession Act, 1956. Parts of this Act was amended in 2005 by the Hindu Succession (Amendment) Act, 2005.Creation of Hindu Law under which all major members of the family get right by birth in the ancestral property of the family.

HUF property is managed by senior most major male member called 'Manager' or 'Karta'. Upon death of Karta, next senior male coparcener becomes Karta. Joint owners of HUF are known as coparceners. It consists of one common living ancestor and his all male & female (female included from Sept. 2005) descendent up to three generations next to him. HUF cannot enter into a partnership as per Supreme Court judgement of 1998.

HUF account is operated by Karta. Karta has authority to borrow money for the family necessities & for ancestral family business. Documents are to be executed by Karta. All major coparceners are to be made guarantors. The liability of the 'Karta' is unlimited, whereas the liability of the coparceners is limited to their shares in the joint family estate.

Details/documents required for opening a HUF bank account

- A copy of the PAN card in the name of HUF
- A copy of the PAN card of Karta/authorized signatory
- Passport size photographs of the Karta/authorized signatory
- Proof of Identity of the Karta/authorized signatory (e.g. PAN, Passport, Aadhar, driving license, voter's ID card, etc) [It is mandatory to link the Aadhaar of Karta with PAN of HUF]
- Proof of address of the Karta/authorized signatory (e.g. Passport, Aadhar, driving license, voter's ID card, electricity bill, etc)
- Details such as the mobile number/phone number/ e-mail address of the Karta/authorized signatory are taken.
- A declaration that states that Karta/authorized signatory will open and operate the bank account. This declaration will be signed by Karta and two or more major co-parceners of HUF. Generally, this declaration is included in the account opening form only by the banks.

3. Sole Proprietary Firms

Business is wholly owned by an individual. In law, there is no difference between proprietor & the firm. In all respects, it is an account in the name of an individual only except that it is operated upon by the proprietor on behalf of firm. The firm should have PAN or GST Number. Proprietorship letter in bank's Performa is to be obtained. Proof of proprietorship firm to be obtained. Creditors have recourse not only against assets of the firm but also against private assets of the proprietor. Proprietor can authorize another person to operate the account through Mandate or Power of Attorney.

For opening an account in the name of a sole proprietary firm, CDD of the individual (proprietor) shall be carried out. In addition to the above, any two of the following documents as a proof of business/ activity in the name of the proprietary firm shall also be obtained:

- Registration certificate

- Certificate/licence issued by the municipal authorities under Shop and Establishment Act.
- Sales and income tax returns.
- CST/VAT/ GST certificate (provisional/final).
- Certificate/registration document issued by Sales Tax/Service Tax/ Professional Tax authorities.
- IEC (Importer Exporter Code) issued to the proprietary concern by the office of DGFT or Licence/certificate of practice issued in the name of the proprietary concern by any professional body incorporated under a statute.
- Complete Income Tax Return (not just the acknowledgement) in the name of the sole proprietor where the firm's income is reflected, duly acknowledged by the Income Tax authorities.
- As address proof Utility bills such as electricity, water, landline telephone bills, etc.
- In cases where the Regulated Entities (REs) are satisfied that it is not possible to furnish two such documents, Regulated Entities (REs) may, at their discretion, accept only one of those documents as proof of business/activity.
- Provided Regulated Entities (REs) undertake contact point verification and collect such other information and clarification as would be required to establish the existence of such firm, and shall confirm and satisfy itself that the business activity has been verified from the address of the proprietary concern.
- Foreign Account Tax Compliance Act (FATCA) declaration.

4. Partnership Firm

Partnership is the relation between persons who have agreed to share profits of business carried on by all or any one them acting for all (Indian Partnership Act 1932). As per RBI instruction now Registration Certificate and Partnership deed to be obtained.

As per Indian Companies Act 2013, Maximum number of partner can be up to 100 in a firm (Earlier number of partner was restricted to 20 for other businesses & 10 for banking business).

Partnership is not a distinct legal person from the partners who have made partnership firm. HUF cannot enter into a partnership as per Supreme Court judgement of 1998. The firm should have PAN or GST Number. A partner cannot delegate his authority to operate the account.

A minor cannot be a partner, but he can be admitted for his benefit in an existing partnership firm. The particulars of minor partner, particularly the DOB should be properly recorded.

In case of death/retirement/insolvency of a partner account should be stopped, if the balance is in debit and a fresh account should opened after fresh sanction of limit. In case of dispute when one partner revokes the authority against the other partner, operation in the account should be stopped.

Dissolution of the Partnership firm can take place by following ways:

- By mutual consent;
- Death/insolvency/retirement of a partner;
- Operation of Law (insolvency of all partners, business becoming unlawful, dissolution by a competent court; and
- In case of automatic dissolution.

Basic documents required for opening Partnership account are as follows

- Partnership Deed.
- PAN Card in the Name of the Partnership Firm.
- Address Proof of the Partnership Firm.
- Identity Proof of all Partners.
- Partnership Registration Certificate (if Registered Partnership)

5. Limited Liability Partnership (LLP)

A limited liability partnership (LLP) is a partnership in which some or all partners (depending on the jurisdiction) have limited liabilities. LLP is governed by limited liability partnership Act 2008. Liability is limited to the extent of his contribution in the LLP. Minimum 2 designated partner and no limit on maximum number of Partners. A partner is not liable for another partner's misconduct or negligence, except in certain cases. LLP is a legal entity separate from its partner.

It has own assets in his name, sure and be sued. Since LLP contains element of both 'a corporate structure' as well as 'a partnership firm structure' LLP is called a hybrid between a company and a partnership. It has perpetual succession (death of a partner does not affect the existence of LLP). Partners have a right to manage the business directly. Firms and companies can get themselves converted into LLP. LLP cannot raise fund from public.

Basic documents required for opening LLP account are as follows

- Certificate of Registration of the LLP issued by registrar
- Communication of address proof of the LLP if it is different from the address mentioned on the Certificate of Registration
- Current landline/ mobile number and e-mail ID of the LLP
- Permanent Account Number (PAN) of the entity
- Board resolution
- Latest passport-size colour photograph of each of the authorized signatories
- A copy of one valid photo identification and address proof of each of the authorized signatories
- In case POA has been granted for account operations – photograph, identity and address proof of the POA holder should also be submitted along with the POA agreement
- Shareholding pattern/ list of beneficial owners holding more than 15% in the company either directly or indirectly (must be on letterhead).
- PAN/ identity proof of such beneficial owners as identified above.
- Address proof of beneficial owners as identified above.
- LLP deed agreement and LLP letter
- Updated list of designated partners.
- Foreign Account Tax Compliance Act (FATCA) declaration.

6. Companies

Companies are defined in Indian Company Act 1956. As per the provision of Company Act 2013 (implemented with effect from 1st April 2014), recognizes a joint Stock Company is a legal person with perpetual entity & is distinct from its members. A company or association of persons can be created at law as legal person so that the company in itself can accept limited liability for civil responsibility. Because companies are legal persons, they also may associate and register themselves as companies otherwise it will be treated as illegal. Address of the registered office is compulsory. It is the address at which all the documents & notices may be served upon the company. Cheques favouring company are not to be credited to the personal accounts of the Directors or other officers of the company.

Following documents are required for account opening of a company:

- **Certificate of Incorporation:** Issued by Registrar of Companies. It is conclusive proof for incorporation of the company & compliance of all formalities by promoters.
- **Certificate of commencement of business:** A company having share capital cannot commence business until it has obtained the certificate to commence business (COB) from the concerned Registrar of Companies. Certificate of commencement of business is not required by Private Ltd. Co. as its shares are closely held & it can commence business on its incorporation.
- **Memorandum of Association:** Company's fundamental & unalterable law. Embodies Company's name, Authorized capital, Objectives of the company, Liability of shareholders.
- **Article of Association:** Regulations controlling internal management of the company. Rights & powers of the Directors, rules about conduct of company meetings & business, Procedure for borrowing & limit on borrowing etc.
- **Copy of Board Resolution:** Certified copy of Board Resolution authorizing to borrow from the Bank with details of limit, security etc., Persons who are authorized to sign the security documents & operate the Bank Account, persons in whose presence Seal of the company will be affixed to the security documents.
- **Company identification Number (CIN):** As per RBI guidelines Company Identification Number (CIN) assigned by the ROC is now compulsory for opening of bank account of the company
- **Company common Seal:** Common seal if any, of the company available should be embossed on bank`s documents. As per Companies (Amendment) Act, 2015 and RBI instruction Company Common Seal is not necessary, if other documents available during current account opening.
- **Ultimate Beneficial Owner (UBO) declaration**: If an individual has 25% or more of shareholding or capital or profits in the company, the individual should identify as an ultimate beneficiary and submit Ultimate Beneficial Owner (UBO) declaration.
- **FATCA declaration:** Foreign Account Tax Compliance Act (FATCA) declaration.

Different types of companies in India

I) Private Company:

Private Company has shareholders with limited liability and its shares may not be offered to the general public. Private Limited Company having a no minimum paid-up share capital limitation now. (As per Companies (Amendment) Act, 2015, paid-up share capital of one lakh rupee or such higher paid-up share capital as may be prescribed is omitted now). It has minimum two members and maximum member restricted to two hundred and Minimum two directors and no maximum number of directors is restricted.

b) Public Company:

Public company means a company which is not a private company and has no minimum paid-up share capital limitation now (As per Companies (Amendment) Act, 2015, paid-up share capital of five lakh rupee or such higher paid-up share capital as may be prescribed is omitted now). Shares are offered to the public & are listed on stock exchange. Minimum seven members no limit of maximum number. Minimum three directors maximum fifteen director limits. Provided, that a company may appoint more than fifteen directors after passing a special resolution (As per Companies Act 2013, no Central Government permission required now). At least one-woman director shall be on Board. Certificate of commencement of business is must to do any type of business.

c) Government Company:

Government Company means any company in which not less than fifty one percent. Of paid-up share capital is held by the Central Government, or by any State Government, or partly by the Central Government and partly by one or more State Governments and includes a company which is a subsidiary company of such a Government company.

d) One Person Company:

The Companies Act 2013 Act introduces a new type of entity to the existing list i.e. apart from forming a public or private limited company, the 2013 act enables the formation of a new entity a 'one-person company' (OPC). An OPC means a company with only one person having a sole member [section 3(1) of 2013 Act]. An OPC can be formed only by an Indian Resident and citizen.

e) Other Companies:

As per Companies act 1956, companies can be classified on the basis of time, place of incorporation and nature of working share capital as follows:

- **Foreign Company:** It means a company incorporated outside India and having a place of business in India whether by itself or through an agent, physically or through electronic mode and conduct any business activity in India in any other manner.
- **Existing Company:** A company which is established before the Company Act 1956 is called Existing Company.
- **Holding Company:** A company is known as the holding company of another company if it has control over another company.
- **Subsidiary Company:** A company is known as subsidiary of another company when control is exercised by the latter over the former called a subsidiary company. A company is to be deemed to be subsidiary company of another.

7. Trust

Trusts are governed by the Indian Trust Act, 1882. A trust is created when ownership of a property is transferred to someone for holding or managing it for benefit of another person(s). Trust may be public charitable trust or private trust (for benefit of private individuals). Trusts managed by trustees. Loan can be granted if it is for the purpose of the trust. Trustee is authorized to borrow as per the trust deed. Original Trust Deed to be examined before financing. Certificate of Registration under Public Trust Act to be examined & copy to be kept on record.

Savings Account can be opened for Trusts/NGOs in accordance with the RBI Guidelines vide circular number RBI/2015-16/39 DBR.No.Dir.BC.7/ 13.03.00/2015-16)

Entities eligible for maintaining Savings Account under Trust/NGO segment are

- Primary Co-operative Credit Society (which is being financed by the bank)
- Khadi and Village Industries Boards
- Agriculture Produce Market Committees
- Societies registered under the Societies Registration Act, 1860 or any other corresponding law in force in State or a Union Territory (except societies registered under the State Co-operative Societies Acts and specific state enactment creating Land Mortgage Banks)
- Section 25 Companies (as per Companies Act, 1956) or Section 8 Companies (as per Companies Act,2013)

- Institutions/entities whose entire income is exempt from payment of Income-tax under Income-Tax Act, 1961
- Government departments/bodies/agencies in respect of grants/ subsidies released for implementation of various programmes/ schemes sponsored by Central/State Government (subject to production of an authorization from the respective Government departments to open savings bank account)
- Development of Women and Children in Rural Areas (DWCRA)
- Self-help Groups (SHGs), registered or unregistered, which are engaged in promoting savings habits among their members
- Farmers' Clubs - Vikas Volunteer Vahini – VVV

Documentations required for opening Savings Account of Trust/NGO

- Registration Certificate of Trust / Society / Association/ Club
- Trust Deed / Bye-laws / Constitutional Document (If unregistered, notarized copy to be obtained)
- Copy of PAN Card
- Income Tax registration u/s 12A for entities as specified in RBI circular
- Certified copy of resolution for opening and operating of the account
- Duly authenticated list of current Trustees / Office bearers on the letter head of the entity
- Address proof of the entity
- Beneficial Ownership declaration
- KYC documents of the authorized signatories

8. Clubs & Societies

Clubs & Societies are non-profit making organization and represent a group of persons. These are normally incorporated under Cooperative Society Act. Clubs can be registered under Society Act 1860, or Company Act 1956. These get the status of a legal entity only after their incorporation in their own name. These are governed by rules & regulations (bye laws).

General Documentation for opening Savings Account of Trust/NGO

- Registration Certificate of Trust / Society / Association/ Club
- Trust Deed / Bye-laws / Constitutional Document (If unregistered, notarized copy to be obtained)
- Copy of PAN Card

- Income Tax registration u/s 12A for entities as specified in RBI circular
- Certified copy of resolution for opening and operating of the account
- Duly authenticated list of current Trustees / Office bearers on the letter head of the entity
- Address proof of the entity
- Beneficial Ownership declaration
- KYC documents of the authorized signatories

Note: ***For all type of above discussed accounts documentary requirements for opening a bank account may differ from bank to bank. But for most banks, the above list of documents should suffice the purpose.***

CHAPTER FIFTEEN

NEGOTIABLE INSTRUMENTS ACT, 1881

Negotiable Instruments Act, 1881 is an act in India dating from the British colonial rule, that is still in force largely unchanged.

History

The history of the present Act is a long one. The Act was originally drafted in 1866 by the 3rd Indian Law Commission and introduced in December 1867 in the Council and it was referred to a Select Committee. Objections were raised by the mercantile community to the numerous deviations from the English Law in which it contained. The Bill had to be redrafted in 1877. After the lapse of a sufficient period for criticism by the Local Governments, the High Courts and the chambers of commerce, the Bill was revised by a Select Committee. In spite of this Bill could not reach the final stage. In 1880 by the Order of the Secretary of State, the Bill had to be referred to a new Law Commission. On the recommendation of the new Law Commission, the Bill was re-drafted and again it was sent to a Select Committee which adopted most of the additions recommended by the new Law Commission. The draft thus prepared for the fourth time was introduced in the Council and was passed into law in 1881 being the Negotiable Instruments Act, 1881 (Act No.26 of 1881).

The most important class of Credit Instruments that evolved in India were termed Hundi. Their use was most widespread in the twelfth century and has continued till today. In a sense, they represent the oldest surviving form of credit instrument. These were used in trade and credit transactions;

they were used as remittance instruments for the purpose of transfer of funds from one place to another. In Modern era Hundi served as traveller's cheques.

According to Section 13 of the Negotiable Instruments Act, "A negotiable instrument means a promissory note, bill of exchange or cheque payable either to order or to bearer.' But in Section 1, it is also described that Local extent, Saving of usage relating to hundis, etc., Commencement. -It extends to the whole of India but nothing herein contained affects the Indian Paper Currency Act, 1871, Section 21, or affects any local usage relating to any instrument in an oriental language. Provided that such usages may be excluded by any words in the body of the instrument, which indicate an intention that the legal relations of the parties thereto shall be governed by this Act; and it shall come

Main Types of Negotiable Instruments are:

Inland Instruments

Foreign Instruments

Bank

Finance companies(listed) Draft

Modern day

We prefer to carry a small piece of paper known as Cheque rather than carrying the currency worth the value of the Cheque. Before 1988 there being no provision to restrain the person issuing the Cheque without having sufficient funds in his account. Of course on Dishonoured cheque there is a civil liability accrued. In order to ensure promptitude and remedy against the defaulters of the Negotiable Instrument a criminal remedy of penalty was inserted in Negotiable Instruments Act, 1881 by amending it with Negotiable Instruments Act, 1988.

With the insertion of these provisions in the Act the situation certainly improved and the instances of dishonour have relatively come down but on account of application of different interpretative techniques by different High Courts on different provisions of the Act it further compounded and complicated the situation although on dishonour of cheques the trends of the verdicts of the Supreme Court of India

Parliament enacted the Negotiable Instruments (Amendment and Miscellaneous Provisions) Act, 2002 (55 of 2002), which is intended to plug the loopholes. This amendment Act inserts five new sections from 143 to 147 touching various limbs of the parent Act and Cheque truncation through digitally were also included and the amendment Act was into force on February 6, 2003.

Review and Reform

In June 2020, the Finance Ministry in the Government of India proposed the decriminalisation of a number of white-collar crimes, including cheque bouncing under Section 138 of the Negotiable Instruments Act, in order to improve the ease of doing business as well as to reduce imprisonment rates. The proposal has been opposed by a number of trade and business associations, including the Confederation of All-India Traders (CAIT), the Indian Banks' Association and Finance Industry Development Council (FIDC), and the Federation of Industrial and Commercial Organisation (FICO).

CHAPTER SIXTEEN

Objectives of Negotiable Instruments Act

After reading this lesson, you should be able to-

• Understand meaning, essential characteristics and types of negotiable instruments;

• Describe the meaning and marketing of cheques, crossing of cheques and cancellation of crossing of a cheque;

• Explain capacity and liability parties to a negotiable instruments; and

• Understand various provisions of negotiable instrument Act, 1881 regarding negotiation, assignment, endorsement, acceptance, etc. of negotiable instruments.

CHAPTER SEVENTEEN

INTRODUCTION

The Negotiable Instruments Act was enacted, in India, in 1881. Prior to its enactment, the provision of the English Negotiable Instrument Act were applicable in India, and the present Act is also based on the English Act with certain modifications. It extends to the whole of India except the State of Jammu and Kashmir. The Act operates subject to the provisions of Sections 31 and 32 of the Reserve Bank of India Act, 1934.

Section 31 of the Reserve Bank of India Act provides that no person in India other than the Bank or as expressly authorized by this Act, the Central Government shall draw, accept, make or issue any bill of exchange, hundi, promissory note or engagement for the payment of money payable to bearer on demand. This Section further provides that no one except the RBI or the Central Government can make or issue a promissory note expressed to be payable or demand or after a certain time. Section 32 of the Reserve Bank of India Act makes issue of such bills or notes punishable with fine which may extend to the amount of the instrument. The effect or the consequences of these provisions are:

1. A promissory note cannot be made payable to the bearer, no matter whether it is payable on demand or after a certain time.

2. A bill of exchange cannot be made payable to the bearer on demand though it can be made payable to the bearer after a certain time.

3. But a cheque {though a bill of exchange} payable to bearer or demand can be drawn on a person's account with a banker.

CHAPTER EIGHTEEN

MEANING & CHARACTERISTICS OF NEGOTIABLE INSTRUMENTS

MEANING OF NEGOTIABLE INSTRUMENTS

According to Section 13 (a) of the Act, "Negotiable instrument means a promissory note, bill of exchange or cheque payable either to order or to bearer, whether the word "order" or " bearer" appear on the instrument or not."In the words of Justice, Willis, "A negotiable instrument is one, the property in which is acquired by anyone who takes it bonafide and for value notwithstanding any defects of the title in the person from whom he took it".

Thus, the term, negotiable instrument means a written document which creates a right in favour of some person and which is freely transferable. Although the Act mentions only these three instruments (such as a promissory note, a bill of exchange and cheque), it does not exclude the possibility of adding any other instrument which satisfies the following two conditions of negotiability:

1. The instrument should be freely transferable (by delivery or by endorsement. and delivery) by the custom of the trade; and

2. The person who obtains it in good faith and for value should get it free from all defects, and be entitled to recover the money of the instrument in his own name. As such, documents like share warrants payable to bearer, debentures payable to bearer and dividend warrants are negotiable

instruments. But the money orders and postal orders, deposit receipts, share certificates, bill of lading, dock warrant, etc. are not negotiable instruments. Although they are transferable by delivery and endorsements, yet they are not able to give better title to the bonafide transferee for value than what the transferor has.

CHARACTERISTICS OF A NEGOTIABLE INSTRUMENT

A negotiable instrument has the following characteristics:

1. Property: The possessor of the negotiable instrument is presumed to be the owner of the property contained therein. A negotiable instrument does not merely give possession of the instrument but right to property also.

The property in a negotiable instrument can be transferred without any formality. In the case of bearer instrument, the property passes by mere delivery to the transferee. In the case of an order instrument, endorsement and delivery are required for the transfer of property.

2. Title: The transferee of a negotiable instrument is known as 'holder in due course.' A bona fide transferee for value is not affected by any defect of title on the part of the transferor or of any of the previous holders of the instrument.

3. Rights: The transferee of the negotiable instrument can sue in his own name, in case of dishonour. A negotiable instrument can be transferred any number of times till it is at maturity. The holder of the instrument need not give notice of transfer to the party liable on the instrument to pay.

4. Presumptions: Certain presumptions apply to all negotiable instruments e.g., a presumption that consideration has been paid under it. It is not necessary to write in a promissory note the words 'for value received' or similar expressions because the payment of consideration is presumed. The words are usually included to create additional evidence of consideration.

5. Prompt payment: A negotiable instrument enables the holder to expect prompt payment because dishonour means the ruin of the credit of all persons who are parties to the instrument.

CHAPTER NINETEEN

Presumptions as to Negotiable Instrument

Sections 118 and 119 of the Negotiable Instrument Act lay down certain presumptions which the court presumes in regard to negotiable instruments. In other words these presumptions need not be proved as they are presumed to exist in every negotiable instrument. Until the contrary is proved the following presumptions shall be made in case of all negotiable instruments:

1. Consideration: It shall be presumed that every negotiable instrument was made drawn, accepted or endorsed for consideration. It is presumed that, consideration is present in every negotiable instrument until the contrary is presumed. The presumption of consideration however may be rebutted by proof that the instrument had been obtained from its lawful owner by means of fraud or undue influence.

2. Date: Where a negotiable instrument is dated, the presumption is that it has been made or drawn on such date, unless the contrary is proved.

3. Time of acceptance: Unless the contrary is proved, every accepted bill of exchange is presumed to have been accepted within a reasonable time after its issue and before its maturity. This presumption only applies when the acceptance is not dated; if the acceptance bears a date, it will prima facie be taken as evidence of the date on which it was made.

4. Time of transfer: Unless the contrary is presumed it shall be presumed that every transfer of a negotiable instrument was made before its maturity.

5. Order of endorsement: Until the contrary is proved it shall be presumed that the endorsements appearing upon a negotiable instrument were made in the order in which they appear thereon.

6. Stamp: Unless the contrary is proved, it shall be presumed that a lost promissory note, bill of exchange or cheque was duly stamped.

7. Holder in due course: Until the contrary is proved, it shall be presumed that the holder of a negotiable instrument is the holder in due course. Every holder of a negotiable instrument is presumed to have paid consideration for it and to have taken it in good faith. But if the instrument was obtained from its lawful owner by means of an offence or fraud, the holder has to prove that he is a holder in due course.

8. Proof of protest: Section 119 lays down that in a suit upon an instrument which has been dishonoured, the court shall on proof of the protest, presume the fact of dishonour, unless and until such fact is disproved.

CHAPTER TWENTY

Types of Negotiable Instrument

Section 13 of the Negotiable Instruments Act states that a negotiable instrument is a promissory notes, bill of exchange or a cheque payable either to order or to bearer.

Negotiable instruments recognized by statute are:

i. Promissory notes
ii. Bills of exchange
iii. Cheques.

Negotiable instruments recognized by usage or custom are:

i. Hundis
ii. Share warrants
iii. Dividend warrants
iv. Bankers draft
v. Circular notes
vi. Bearer debentures
vii. Debentures of Bombay Port Trust
viii. Railway receipts
ix. Delivery orders.

This list of negotiable instrument is not a closed chapter. With the growth of commerce, new kinds of securities may claim recognition as negotiable instruments. The courts in India usually follow the practice of English courts in according the character of negotiability to other instruments.

1) Promissory Notes : Section 4 of the Act defines, "A promissory note is an instrument in writing (note being a bank-note or a currency note) containing an unconditional undertaking, signed by the maker, to pay a certain sum of money to or to the order of a certain person, or to the bearer of the instruments."

Essential elements

An instrument to be a promissory note must possess the following elements:

1. It must be in writing: A mere verbal promise to pay is not a promissory note. The method of writing (either in ink or pencil or printing, etc.) is unimportant, but it must be in any form that cannot be altered easily.

2. It must certainly an express promise or clear understanding to pay: There must be an express undertaking to pay. A mere acknowledgment is not enough.

The following are not promissory notes as there is no promise to pay.

If A writes:

a. "Mr. B, I.O.U. (I owe you) Rs. 500"
b. "I am liable to pay you Rs. 500".
c. "I have taken from you Rs. 100, whenever you ask for it has / have to pay".

The following will be taken as promissory notes because there is an express promise to pay

If A writes:

(a) "I promise to pay B or order Rs. 500"

(b) "I acknowledge myself to be indebted to B in Rs. 1000 to be paid on demand, for the value received".

(3) Promise to pay must be unconditional: A conditional undertaking destroys the negotiable character of an otherwise negotiable instrument. Therefore, the promise to pay must not depend upon the happening of some outside contingency or event. It must be payable absolutely.

(4) It should be signed by the maker: The person who promises to pay must sign the instrument even though it might have been written by the promisor himself. There are no restrictions regarding the form or place of signatures in the instrument. It may be in any part of the instrument. It may be in pencil or ink, a thumb mark or initials. The pronote can be signed by

the authorized agent of the maker, but the agent must expressly state as to on whose behalf he is signing, otherwise he himself may be held liable as a maker. The only legal requirement is that it should indicate with certainty the identity of the person and his intention to be bound by the terms of the agreement.

(5) The maker must be certain: The note self must show clearly who the person is agreeing to undertake the liability to pay the amount. In case a person signs in an assumed name, he is liable as a maker because a maker is taken as certain if from his description sufficient indication follows about his identity. In case two or more persons promise to pay, they may bind themselves jointly or jointly and severally, but their liability cannot be in the alternative.

(6) The payee must be certain: The instrument must point out with certainty the person to whom the promise has been made. The payee may be ascertained by name or by designation. A note payable to the maker himself is not pronate unless it is indorsed by him. In case, there is a mistake in the name of the payee or his designation; the note is valid, if the payee can be ascertained by evidence. Even where the name of a dead person is entered as payee in ignorance of his death, his legal representative can enforce payment.

(7) The promise should be to pay money and money only: Money means legal tender money and not old and rare coins. A promise to deliver paddy either in the alternative or in addition to money does not constitute a promissory note.

(8) The amount should be certain: One of the important characteristics of a promissory note is certainty—not only regarding the person to whom or by whom payment is to be made but also regarding the amount.

However, paragraph 2 of Section 5 provides that the sum does not become indefinite merely because

(a) There is a promise to pay amount with interest at a specified rate.

(b) The amount is to be paid at an indicated rate of exchange.

(c) The amount is payable by installments with a condition that the whole balance shall fall due for payment on a default being committed in the payment of anyone installment.

(9) Other formalities: The other formalities regarding number, place, date, consideration etc. though usually found given in the promissory notes but are not essential in law. The date of instrument is not material unless the amount is made payable at a certain time after date. Even in such a

case, omission of date does not invalidate the instrument and the date of execution can be independently ascertained and proved.

On demand (or six month after date) I promise to pay Peter or order the sum of rupees one thousand with interest at Eight percent per annum until payment.

2) Bill of exchange : Section 5 of the Act defines, "A bill of exchange is an instrument in writing containing an unconditional order, signed by the maker, directing a certain person to pay a certain sum of money only to, or to the order of a certain person or to the bearer of the instrument".

A bill of exchange, therefore, is a written acknowledgement of the debt, written by the creditor and accepted by the debtor. There are usually three parties to a bill of exchange drawer, acceptor or drawee and payee. Drawer himself may be the payee.

Essential conditions of a bill of exchange

(1) It must be in writing.

(2) It must be signed by the drawer.

(3) The drawer, drawee and payee must be certain.

(4) The sum payable must also be certain.

(5) It should be properly stamped.

(6) It must contain an express order to pay money and money alone.

For example, in the following cases, there is no order to pay, but only a request to pay. Therefore, none can be considered as a bill of exchange:

(a) "I shall be highly obliged if you make it convenient to pay Rs.1000 to Suresh".

(b) "Mr. Rajesh, please let the bearer have one thousand rupees, and place it to my account and oblige"

However, there is an order to pay, though it is politely made, in the following examples:

(a) "Please pay Rs. 500 to the order of 'A'.

(b) 'Mr. A will oblige Mr. C, by paying to the order of' P".

(7) The order must be unconditional.

Distinction between bill of exchange and Promissory Note

1. Number of parties: In a promissory note there are only two parties – the maker (debtor) and the payee (creditor). In a bill of exchange, there are three parties; drawer, drawee and payee; although any two out of the three may be filled by one and the same person,

2. Payment to the maker: A promissory note cannot be made payable the maker himself, while in a bill of exchange to the drawer and payee or drawee and payee may be same person.

3. Unconditional promise: A promissory note contains an unconditional promise by the maker to pay to the payee or his order, whereas in a bill of exchange, there is an unconditional order to the drawee to pay according to the direction of the drawer.

4. Prior acceptance: A note is presented for payment without any prior acceptance by the maker. A bill of exchange is payable after sight must be accepted by the drawee or someone else on his behalf, before it can be presented for payment.

5. Primary or absolute liability: The liability of the maker of a promissory note is primary and absolute, but the liability of the drawer of a bill of exchange is secondary and conditional.

6. Relation: The maker of the promissory note stands in immediate relation with the payee, while the maker or drawer of an accepted bill stands in immediate relations with the acceptor and not the payee.

7. Protest for dishonour: Foreign bill of exchange must be protested for dishonour when such protest is required to be made by the law of the country where they are drawn, but no such protest is needed in the case of a promissory note.

8. Notice of dishonour: When a bill is dishonoured, due notice of dishonour is to be given by the holder to the drawer and the intermediate indorsers, but no such notice need be given in the case of a note.

Classification of Bills

Bills can be classified as:

(1) Inland and foreign bills.

(2) Time and demand bills.

(3) Trade and accommodation bills.

(1) Inland and Foreign Bills

Inland bill: A bill is, named as an inland bill if:

(a) It is drawn in India on a person residing in India, whether payable in or outside India, or

(b) It is drawn in India on a person residing outside India but payable in India.

The following are the Inland bills

(i) A bill is drawn by a merchant in Delhi on a merchant in Madras. It is payable in Bombay. The bill is an inland bill.

(ii) A bill is drawn by a Delhi merchant on a person in London, but is made payable in India. This is an inland bill.

(iii) A bill is drawn by a merchant in Delhi on a merchant in Madras. It is accepted for payment in Japan. The bill is an inland bill.

Foreign Bill: A bill which is not an inland bill is a foreign bill. The following are the foreign bills:

(a) A bill drawn outside India and made payable in India.

(b) A bill drawn outside India on any person residing outside India.

(c) A bill drawn in India on a person residing outside India and made payable outside India.

(d) A bill drawn outside India on a person residing in India.

(e) A bill drawn outside India and made payable outside India.

Bills in sets (Section 132 and 133): The foreign bills are generally drawn in sets of three, and each sets is termed as a 'via'. As soon as anyone of the set is paid, the others become inoperative. These bills are drawn in different parts. They are drawn in order to avoid their loss or miscarriage during transit. Each part is dispatched separately. To avoid delay, all the parts are sent on the same day; by different mode of conveyance.

Sections 132 and 133 provide for the following rules:

(i) A bill of exchange may be drawn in parts, each part being numbered and containing a provision that it shall continue payable only so long as the others remain unpaid. All parts make one bill and the entire bill is extinguished, i.e. when payment is made on one part- the other parts will become inoperative (Section 132).

(ii) The drawer should sign and deliver all the parts but the acceptance is to be conveyed only on one of the parts. In case a person accepts or endorses different parts of the bill in favour of different persons, he and the subsequent endorsers of each part are liable on such part as if it were a separate bill (Section 132).

(iii) As between holders in due course of the different parts of the same bill, he who first acquired title to anyone part is entitled to the other parts and is also entitled to claim the money represented by bill (Section 133).

(2) Time and Demand Bill

Time bill: A bill payable after a fixed time is termed as a time bill. In other words, bill payable "after date" is a time bill.

Demand bill: A bill payable at sight or on demand is termed as a demand bill.

(3) Trade and Accommodation Bill

Trade bill: A bill drawn and accepted for a genuine trade transaction is termed as a "trade bill".

Accommodation bill: A bill drawn and accepted not for a genuine trade transaction but only to provide financial help to some party is termed as an "accommodation bill".

Example: A, is need of money for three months. He induces his friend B to accept a bill of exchange drawn on him for Rs.10,000/- for three months. The bill is drawn and accepted. The bill is an "accommodation bill". A may get the bill discounted from his bankers immediately, paying a small sum as discount. Thus, he can use the funds for three months and then just before maturity he may remit the money to B, who will meet the bill on maturity.

In the above example A is the "accommodated party" while B is the "accommodating party".

It is to be noted that a recommendation bill may be for accommodation of both the drawer arid acceptor. In such a case, they share the proceeds of the discounted bill.

Rules regarding accommodation bills are:

(i) In case the patty accommodated continues to hold the bill till maturity, the accommodating party shall not be liable to him for payment of, the bill since the contract between them is not based on any consideration (Section 43).

(ii) But the accommodating party shall be liable to any subsequent holder for value who may be knowing the exact position that the bill is an accommodation bill and that the full consideration has not been received by the acceptor. The accommodating party can, in turn, claim compensation from the accommodated party for the amount it has been asked to pay the holder for value.

(iii) An accommodation bill may be negotiated after maturity. The holder or such a bill after maturity is in the same position as a holder before maturity; provided he takes it in good faith and for value (Section 59)

In form and all other respects an accommodation bill is quite similar to an ordinary bill of exchange. There is nothing on the face of the accommodation bill to distinguish it from an ordinary trade bill.

3) Cheques :Section 6 of the Act defines "A cheque is a bill of exchange drawn on a specified banker, and not expressed to be payable otherwise than on demand".

A cheque is bill of exchange with two more qualifications, namely,

i. It is always drawn on a specified banker, and
ii. It is always payable on demand.

Consequently, all cheque are bill of exchange, but all bills are not cheque. A cheque must satisfy all the requirements of a bill of exchange; that is, it must be signed by the drawer, and must contain an unconditional order on a specified banker to pay a certain sum of money to or to the order of a certain person or to the bearer of the cheque. It does not require acceptance.

Distinction between Bills of Exchange and Cheque

1. A bill of exchange is usually drawn on some person or firm, while a cheque is always drawn on a bank.

2. It is essential that a bill of exchange must be accepted before its payment can be claimed. A cheque does not require any such acceptance.

3. A cheque can only be drawn payable on demand; a bill may be also drawn payable on demand, or on the expiry of a certain period after date or sight.

4. A grace of three days is allowed in the case of time bills while no grace is given in the case of a cheque.

5. The drawer of the bill is discharged from his liability, if it is not presented for payment, but the drawer of a cheque is discharged only if he suffers any damage by delay in presenting the cheque for payment.

6. Notice of dishonour of a bill is necessary, but no such notice is necessary in the case of cheque.

7. A cheque may be crossed, but not needed in the case of bill.

8. A bill of exchange must be properly stamped, while a cheque does not require any stamp.

9. A cheque drawn to bearer payable on demand shall be valid but a bill payable on demand can never be drawn to bearer.

10. Unlike cheques, the payment of a bill cannot be countermanded by the drawer.

4) Hundis : A "Hundi" is a negotiable instrument written in an oriental language. The term hundi includes all indigenous negotiable instruments whether they be in the form of notes or bills.

The word 'hundi' is said to be derived from the Sanskrit word 'hundi', which means "to collect". They are quite popular among the Indian merchants from very old days. They are used to finance trade and commerce and provide a fascile and sound medium of currency and credit.

Hundis are governed by the custom and usage of the locality in which they are intended to be used and not by the provision of the Negotiable Instruments Act. In case there is no customary rule known as to a certain point, the court may apply the provisions of the Negotiable Instruments Act.

It is also open to the parties to expressly exclude the applicability of any custom relating to hundis by agreement.

CHAPTER TWENTY-ONE

Parties to Negotiable Instruments

1) Parties to Bill of exchange

1. Drawer: The maker of a bill of exchange is called the 'drawer'.

2. Drawee: The person directed to pay the money by the drawer is called the 'drawee',

3. Acceptor: After a drawee of a bill has signed his assent upon the bill, or if there are more parts than one, upon one of such pares and delivered the same, or given notice of such signing to the holder or to some person on his behalf, he is called the ' acceptor'.

4. Payee: The person named in the instrument, to whom or to whose order the money is directed to be paid by the instrument is called the 'payee'. He is the real beneficiary under the instrument. Where he signs his name and makes the instrument payable to some other person, that other person does not become the payee.

5. Indorser: When the holder transfers or indorses the instrument to anyone else, the holder becomes the 'indorser'.

6. Indorsee: The person to whom the bill is indorsed is called an 'indorsee'.

7. Holder: A person who is legally entitled to the possession of the negotiable instrument in his own name and to receive the amount thereof, is called a 'holder'. He is either the original payee, or the indorsee. In case the bill is payable to the bearer, the person in possession of the negotiable instrument is called the 'holder'.

8. Drawee in case of need: When in the bill or in any endorsement, the name of any person is given, in addition to the drawee, to be resorted to in case of need, such a person is called 'drawee in case of need'. In such a case it is obligatory on the part of the holder to present the bill to such a drawee in case the original drawee refuses to accept the bill. The bill is taken to be dishonoured by non-acceptance or for nonpayment, only when such a drawee refuses to accept or pay the bill.

9. Acceptor for honour: In case the original drawee refuses to accept the bill or to furnish better security when demanded by the notary, any person who is not liable on the bill, may accept it with the consent of the holder, for the honour of any party liable on the bill. Such an acceptor is called 'acceptor for honour'.

2) Parties to a Promissory Note

1. Maker: He is the person who promises to pay the amount stated in the note. He is the debtor.

2. Payee: He is the person to whom the amount is payable i.e. the creditor.

3. Holder: He is the payee or the person to whom the note might have been indorsed.

4. Indorser & Indorsee: The indorser and indorsee (the same as in the case of a bill).

3) Parties to a Cheque

1. Drawer: He is the person who draws the cheque, i.e., the depositor of money in the bank.

2. Drawee: It is the drawer's banker on whom the cheque has been drawn.

3. Payee: He is the person who is entitled to receive the payment of the cheque.

4. Indorser & Indorsee: The holder, indorser and indorsee (the same as in the case of a bill or note).

Delivery is a voluntary transfer of possession from one person to another. Delivery is essential to complete any contract on a negotiable instrument whether it be contract of making endorsement or acceptance.

The property in the instrument does not pass unless the delivery is fully completed. Section 46 of the Act provides that a negotiable instrument is not made or accepted or endorsed unless it is delivered to a proper person. For instance, if a person signs a promissory note and keeps it with himself, he cannot be said to have made a promissory note; only when it is delivered to the payee that the promissory note is made.

Delivery may be actual or constructive.

Delivery is actual when it is accompanied by actual change of possession of the instrument.

Constructive delivery is effected without any change of actual possession.

CHAPTER TWENTY-FOUR

ENDORSEMENT

ENDORSEMENT : The word 'endorsement' in its literal sense means, writing on the back of an instrument. But under the Negotiable Instruments Act it means, the writing of one's name on the back of the instrument or any paper attached to it with the intention of transferring the rights therein.

Thus, endorsement is signing a negotiable instrument for the purpose of negotiation. The person who effects an endorsement is called an 'endorser', and the person to whom negotiable instrument is transferred by endorsement is called the 'endorsee'.

Essentials of a valid endorsement

The following are the essentials of a valid endorsement:

1. It must be on the instrument. The endorsement may be on the back or face of the instrument and if no space is left on the instrument, it may be made on a separate paper attached to it called allonage. It should usually be in ink.

2. It must be made by the maker or holder of the instrument. A stranger cannot endorse it.

3. It must be signed by the endorser. Full name is not essential. Initials may suffice. Thumb-impression should be attested. Signature may be made on any part of the instrument. A rubber stamp is not accepted but the designation of the holder can be done by a rubber stamp.

4. It may be made either by the endorser merely signing his name on the instrument (it is a blank endorsement) or by any words showing an intention to endorse or transfer the instrument to a specified person (it is an endorsement in full). No specific form of words is prescribed for an endorsement. But intention to transfer must be present. When in a bill or note payable to order the endorsee's name

is wrongly spelt, he should when he endorses it, sign the name as spelt in the instrument and write the correct spelling within brackets after his endorsement.

5. It must be completed by delivery of the instrument. The delivery must be made by the endorser himself or by somebody on his behalf with the intention of passing property therein. Thus, where a person endorses an instrument to another and keeps it in his papers where it is found after his death and then delivered to the endorsee, the latter gets no right on the instrument.

6. It must be an endorsement of the entire bill. A partial endorsement i.e. which purports to transfer to the endorsee a part only of the amount payable does not operate as a valid endorsement.

If delivery is conditional, endorsement is not complete until the condition is fulfilled.

Who may endorse?

The payee of an instrument is the rightful person to make the first endorsement. Thereafter the instrument may be endorsed by any person who has become the holder of the instrument. The maker or the drawer cannot endorse the instrument but if any of them has become the holder thereof he may endorse the instrument. (Section 51).

The maker or drawer cannot endorse or negotiate an instrument unless he is in lawful possession of instrument or is the holder there of.

A payee or indorsee cannot endorse or negotiate unless he is the holder there of.

Classes of endorsement

An endorsement may be:

(1) Blank or general.

(2) Special or full.

(3) Partial.

(4) Restrictive.

(5) Conditional.

(a) Blank or general endorsement (Sections 16 and 54): It is an endorsement when the endorser merely signs on the instrument without mentioning the name of the person in whose favour the endorsement is made. Endorsement in blank specifies no endorsee. It simply consists of the signature of the endorser on the endorsement.

A negotiable instrument even though payable to order becomes a bearer instrument if endorsed in blank. Then it is transferable by mere delivery.

An endorsement in blank may be followed by an endorsement in full.

Example: A bill is payable to X. X endorses the bill by simply affixing his signature. This is an endorsement in blank by X. In this case the bill becomes payable to bearer.

There is no difference between a bill or note indorsed in blank and one payable to bearer. They can both be negotiated by delivery.

(b) Special or full endorsement (Section 16): When the endorsement contains not only the signature of the endorser but also the name of the person in whose favour the endorsement is made, then it is an endorsement in full. Thus, when endorsement is made by writing the words "Pay to A or A's order," followed by the signature of the endorser, it is an endorsement in full. In such an endorsement, it is only the endorsee who can transfer the instrument.

Conversion of endorsement in blank into endorsement in full: When a person receives a negotiable instrument in blank, he may without signing his own name, convert the blank endorsement into an endorsement in full by writing above the endorser's signature a direction to pay to or to the order of himself or some other person. In such a case the person is not liable as the endorser on the bill. In other words, the person transferring such an instrument does not incur all the liabilities of an endorser. (Section 49).

Example: A is the holder of a bill endorsed by B in blank. A writes over B's signature the words "Pay to C or order." A is not liable as endorser but the writing operates as an endorsement in full from B to C.

Where a bill is endorsed in blank, or is payable to bearer and is afterwards endorsed by another in full, the bill remains transferable by delivery with regard to all parties prior to such endorser in full. But such endorser in full cannot be sued by anyone except the person in whose favour the endorsement in full is made. (Section 55).

Example: C the payee of a bill endorses it in blank and delivers it to D, who specially endorses it to E or order. E without endorsement transfers the bill to F. F as the bearer is entitled to receive payment or to sue the drawer, the acceptor, or C who endorsed the bill in blank but he cannot sue D or E.

(c) Partial endorsement (Section 56): A partial endorsement is one which purports to transfer to the endorsee a part only of the amount payable on the instrument. Such an endorsement does not operate as a negotiation of the instrument.

Example: A is the holder of a bill for Rs.1000. He endorses it "pay to B or order Rs.500." This is a partial endorsement and invalid for the purpose of negotiation.

(d) Restrictive endorsement (Section 50): The endorsement of an instrument may contain terms making it restrictive. Restrictive endorsement is one which either by express words restricts or prohibits the further negotiation of a bill or which expresses that it is not a complete and unconditional transfer of the instrument but is a mere authority to the endorsee to deal with bill as directed by such endorsement.

"Pay C," "Pay C for my use," "Pay C for the account of B" are instances of restrictive endorsement. The endorsee under a restrictive endorsement acquires all the rights of the endoser except the right of negotiation.

Conditional or qualified endorsement

It is open to the endorser to annex some condition to his owner liability on the endorsement. An endorsement where the endorsee limits or negatives his liability by putting some condition in the instrument is called a conditional endorsement. A condition imposed by the endorser may be a condition precedent or a condition subsequent. An endorsement which says that the amount will become payable if the endorsee attains majority embodies a condition precedent. A conditional endorsement unlike the restrictive endorsement does not affect the negotiability of the instrument. It is also sometimes called qualified endorsement. An endorsement may be made conditional or qualified in any of the following forms:

(i) 'Sans recourse' endorsement: An endorser may be express word exclude his own liability thereon to the endorser or any subsequent holder in case of dishonour of the instrument. Such an endorsement is called an endorsement sans recourse (without recourse). Thus, 'Pay to A or order sans recourse, 'pay to A or order without recourse to me,' is instances of this type of endorsement. Here if the instrument is dishonoured, the subsequent holder or the indorsee cannot look to the indorser for payment of the same.

An agent signing a negotiable instrument may exclude his personal liability by using words to indicate that he is signing as agent only. The same rule applies to directors of a company signing instruments on behalf of a company. The intention to exclude personal liability must be clear. Where an endorser so excludes his liability and afterwards becomes the holder of the instrument, all intermediate endorsers are liable to him.

Example: A is the holder of a negotiable instrument. Excluding personal liability by an endorsement without recourse, he transfers the instrument to B, and B endorses it to C, who endorses it to A. A can recover the amount of the bill from B and C.

(ii) Facultative endorsement: An endorsement where the endorser extends his liability or abandons some right under a negotiable instrument, is called a facultative endorsement.

"Pay A or order, Notice of dishonour waived" is an example of facultative endorsement.

(iii) 'Sans frais' endorsement: Where the endorser does not want the endorsee or any subsequent holder, to incur any expense on his account on the instrument, the endorsement is 'sans frais'.

(iv) Liability dependent upon a contingency: Where an endorser makes his liability depend upon the happening of a contingent event, or makes the rights of the endorsee to receive the amount depend upon any contingent event, in such a case the liability of the endorser will arise only on the happening of that contingent event.

Thus, an endorser may write 'Pay A or order on his marriage with B'. In such a case, the endorser will not be liable until the marriage takes place and if the marriage becomes impossible, the liability of the endorser comes to an end.

<u>Effects of endorsement</u>

The legal effect of negotiation by endorsement and delivery is:

(i) To transfer property in the instrument from the endorser to the endorsee.

(ii) To vest in the latter the right of further negotiation, and

(iii) A right to sue on the instrument in his own name against all the other parties (Section 50).

<u>Cancellation of endorsement</u>

When the holder of a negotiable instrument, without the consent of the endorser destroys or impairs the endorser's remedy against prior party, the endorser is discharged from liability to the holder to the same extent as if the instrument had been paid at maturity (Section 40).

<u>Negotiation back:</u> 'Negotiation back' is a process under which an endorsee comes again into possession of the instrument in his own right. Where a bill is re-endorsed to a previous endorser, he has no remedy against the intermediate parties to whom he was previously liable though he may further negotiate the bill.

CHAPTER TWENTY-FIVE

INSTRUMENTS WITHOUT CONSIDERATION

INSTRUMENTS WITHOUT CONSIDERATION : A person cannot pass a better title than he himself possesses. A person who is a mere finder of a lost goods or a thief or one who obtains any article by fraud or for an unlawful consideration does not get any title to the thing so acquired. The true owner can recover it not only from him but from any person to whom he may have sold it. But there is a difference between the transfer of ordinary goods and negotiation of negotiable instruments.

The Negotiable Instruments Act provides protection to those persons who acquire the instruments in good faith and for valuable consideration. A holder in due course who has no means to discover the defect of title in an instrument of any previous holder when the instrument may have passed through several hands must be protected if he obtains the instrument for value and in good faith.

Section 58 of the Act provides that no person in possession of an instrument with a defect of title can claim the amount of the instrument unless he is a holder in due course. The moment an instrument comes into the hands of a holder in due course, not only does he get a title which is free from all defects, but having passed through his hands the instrument is cleaned of all defects.

Lost instruments

Where the holder of a bill or note loses it, the finder gets no title to it. The finder cannot lawfully transfer it. The man who lost it can recover it from the finder. But if the instrument is transferable by mere delivery and there is nothing on its face to show that it does not belong to the finder, a holder obtaining it from the finder in good faith and for valuable consideration and before maturity is entitled to the instrument and can recover payment from all the parties thereof. If the instrument is transferable by endorsement, the finder cannot negotiate it except by forging the endorsement.

The holder of the instrument when it is lost must give a notice of loss to all the parties liable on it and also a public notice by advertisement. The holder of a lost bill remains owner in law and as such on maturity can demand payment from the acceptor, and if is dishonoured he must give notice of dishonour to prior parties.

The owner of the lost bill has a right to obtain the duplicate from the drawer and on refusal he can sue the drawer for the same.

Stolen instrument

The position of thief of an instrument is exactly the same as that of a finder of lost instruments. A thief acquires no title to an instrument if he receives payment on it the owner can sue him for the recovery of the amount. But if an instrument payable to bearer is stolen and if transferred to a holder in due course, the owner must suffer.

Instruments obtained by fraud

It is of the essence of all contracts including those on negotiable instruments, that they must have been brought about by free consent of the parties compenent to contract. Any contract to which consent has

been obtained by fraud is voidable at the option of the person whose consent was so obtained. A person who obtains an instrument by fraud gets a defective title. But if such an instrument passes into the hands of a holder in due course, the plea of fraud will not be available against him. If however, it could be shown that a person without negligence on his part was induced to sign an instrument it being represented to him to be a document of a different kind he would not be liable even to a holder in due course.

Instrument obtained for an unlawful consideration

The general rules as to the legality of object or consideration of a contract apply to contracts on negotiable instruments also. An instrument given for an illegal consideration is void and does not covey a valid title to the holder. He cannot enforce payment against any party thereto. Thus, a bill of exchange given in consideration of future illicit cohabitation is void. But if such an instrument passes into the hands of a holder in due course, he obtains a good and complete title to it.

Forged instrument

Forgery confers no title and a holder acquires no title to a forged instrument. A forged instrument is treated as a-nullity. Forgery with the intention of obtaining title to an instrument would include:

(1) Fraudulently writing the name of an existing person,

(2) Signing the name of a fictitious person with the intention that it may pass that of a real person, or

(3) Signing one's own name with the intention that the signature may pass as the signature of some other person of the same name.

Example: A bill is payable to Ram Sunder or order. At maturity it wrongfully comes into the possession of another Ram Sunder who knows that he has no claim on the bill. He puts his own signature and the acceptor pays him. The bill is not discharged and the acceptor remains liable to Ram Sunder who is the owner of the bill.

A forged instrument has no existence in the eyes of law. A title which never came into existence cannot be improved even if it passes into the hands of a holder in due course. A forges B's signature on a promissory note and transfers the same to C who takes it in good faith for value. C gets no title of the note even though he is a holder in due course.

Examples: (a) On a note for Rs.1000, A forges B's signature to it as maker. C, a holder who takes it bonafide and for value acquires no title to the note.

(b) On a bill for Rs.1000 A's acceptance to the bill is forged. The bill comes into hands of B, a bonafide holder for value, B acquires no title to the bill.

Forged endorsement

The case of a forged endorsement is slightly different. If an instrument is endorsed in full, it cannot be negotiated except by an endorsement signed by the person to whom or to whose order the instrument is payable, for the endorsee obtains title only through his endorsement. If an endorsement is forged, the endorsee acquires no title to the instrument even if he is a bonafide purchaser. On the other hand, if the instrument is a bearer instrument or has been endorsed in blank, and there is a forged endorsement the holder gets a good title because holder in such a case derives title by delivery and not by endorsement.

Bankers are specially protected against forged endorsement under Section 85 of the Act.

Examples: (a) A bill is endorsed, "Pay X or order." X must endorse the bill and if his signature is forged, the bill is worthless.

(b) A bill is payable to "X or order." It is stolen from X and the thief forges X's endorsement and endorses it to Y who takes it in good faith and for value. Y acquires no title to the bill.

(c) A bill payable to "A or order" is endorsed in blank by A. It comes into the hands of B. B by simple delivery passes it to C. C forges B's endorsement and transfers it to D. As D does not derive his title through the forged endorsement of B, but through the genuine endorsement of A, he obtains a good title to the instrument in spite of the intervening forged endorsement.

Instrument without consideration

Sections 43 to 45 of the Negotiable Instrument Act deal with the consequences of failure or absence of consideration in negotiable instruments. In the case of negotiable instruments consideration is presumed to exist between the parties unless the contrary is proved. As between immediate parties, if an instrument is made, drawn or endorsed without consideration, or for a consideration which subsequently fails, it is void. As between immediate parties, failure of consideration has the same effect as the absence of consideration. For instance if a promissory note is delivered by the maker to the payee as a gift, it cannot be enforced against such maker.

Examples: (a) C the holder of a bill endorses it in blank to D receiving no value. D for value transfers it by delivery to E. E is a holder of value.

(b) A is the holder of a bill for consideration. A endorses it to B, without consideration. The property in the bill passes to B. The bill is dishonoured at maturity. B cannot sue A on the bill.

As between remote parties, the defence of absence or failure of consideration is not available at all. The holder in due course who has paid consideration can recover it from all prior parties immaterial of the fact whether any of them has received consideration or not. Where there is a partial absence or failure of consideration, as between immediate parties, only that part can be recovered which was actually paid. However, a holder in due course is not affected by this rule. But even between immediate parties, where the part of the consideration which is absent or cannot be ascertained without collateral inquiry, the whole of the amount is recoverable.

Examples: (a) A owes B Rs. 500. B draws a bill on A for Rs. 1000/- . A to accommodate B and at his request accepts it. If B sues A on the bill he can only recover Rs. 500/-.

(b) A draws a bill on B for Rs. 500 payable to the order A. B accepts the bill but subsequently dishonours it by non-payment. A sues B on the bill. B proves that it was accepted for value as to Rs. 400 and as an accommodation to A (the plaintiff) for Rs. 100. A can only recover Rs. 400/- But if this bill gets into the hands of a holder in due course, he can recover the full amount of Rs. 500/.

CHAPTER TWENTY-SIX

HOLDER IN DUE COURSE

HOLDER IN DUE COURSE

Section 9 of the Act defines 'holder in due course' as any person who

i. for valuable consideration,
ii. becomes the possessor of a negotiable instrument payable to bearer or the indorsee or payee thereof,
iii. before the amount mentioned in the document becomes payable, and
iv. Without having sufficient cause to believe that any defect existed in the title of the person from whom he derives his title. (English law does not regard payee as a holder in due course).

The essential qualification of a holder in due course may, therefore, be summed up as follows:

1. He must be a holder for valuable consideration. Consideration must not be void or illegal, e.g. a debt due on a wagering agreement. It may, however, be inadequate. A donee, who acquired title to the instrument by way of gift, is not a holder in due course, since there is no consideration to the contract. He cannot maintain any action against the debtor on the instrument. Similarly, money due on a promissory note executed in consideration of the balance of the security deposit for the lease of a house taken for immoral purposes cannot be recovered by a suit.

2. He must have become a holder (passessor) before the date of maturity of the negotiable instrument. Therefore, a person who takes a bill or promissory note on the day on which it becomes payable cannot

claim rights of a holder in due course because he takes it after it becomes payable, as the bill or note can be discharged at any time on that day.

3. He must have become holder of the negotiable instrument in good faith. Good faith implies that he should not have accepted the negotiable instrument after knowing about any defect in the title to the instrument. But, notice of defect in the title received subsequent to the acquisition of the title will not affect the rights of a holder in due course.

Besides good faith, the Indian Law also requires reasonable care on the part of the holder before he acquires title of the negotiable instrument. He should take the instrument without any negligence on his part. Reasonable care and due caution will be the proper test of his bona fides. It will not be enough to show that the holder acquired the instrument honestly, if in fact, he was negligent or careless. Under conditions of sufficient indications showing the existence of a defect in the title of the transferor, the holder will not become a holder in due course even though he might have taken the instrument without any suspicion or knowledge.

Example:

(i) A bill made out by pasting together pieces of a tom bill taken without enquiry will not make the holder, a holder in due course. It was sufficient to show the intention to cancel the bill. A bill should not be taken without enquiry if suspicion has been aroused.

(ii) A post-dated cheque is not irregular. It will not preclude a bonafide purchase instrument from claiming the rights of a holder in due course. It is to be noted that it is the notice of the defect in the title of his immediate transferor which deprives a person from claiming the right of a holder in due course. Notice of defect in the title of any prior party does not affect the title of the holder.

4. A holder in due course must take the negotiable instrument complete and regular on the face of it.

Privileges of a holder in due course

1. Instrument purged of all defects: A holder in due course who gets the instrument in good faith in the course of its currency is not only himself protected against all defects of title of the person from whom he has received it, but also serves, as a channel to protect all subsequent holders. A holder in due course can recover the amount of the instrument from all previous parties although, as a matter of fact, no consideration was paid by some of the previous parties to instrument or there was a defect of title in the party from whom he took it. Once an instrument passes through the hands of a holder in due course, it is purged of all defects. It is like a current coin. Who-so-ever takes it can recover the amount from all parties previous to such holder (Section 53).

It is to be noted that a holder in due course can purify a defective title but cannot create any title unless the instrument happens to be a bearer one.

Examples:

(i) A obtains Bs acceptance to a bill by fraud. A indorses it to C who takes it as a holder in due course. The instrument is purged of its defects and C gets a good title to it. In case C indorses it to some other person he will also get a good title to it except when he is also a party to the fraud played by A.

(ii) A bill is payable to "A or order". It is stolen from A and the thief forges A's signatures and indorses it to B who takes it as a holder in due course. B cannot recover the money. It is not a case of defective title but a case where title is absolutely absent. The thief does not get any title therefore, cannot transfer any title to it.

(iii) A bill of exchange payable to bearer is stolen. The thief delivers it to B, a holder in due course. B can recover the money of the bill.

2. Rights not affected in case of an inchoate instrument: Right of a holder in due course to recover money is not at all affected even though the instrument was originally an inchoate stamped instrument and the transferor completed the instrument for a sum greater than what was intended by the maker. (Section 20)

3. All prior parties liable: All prior parties to the instrument (the maker or drawer, acceptor and intervening indorers) continue to remain liable to the holder in due course until the instrument is duty Satisfied. The holder in due course can file a suit against the parties liable to pay, in his own name (Section 36)

4. Can enforce payment of a fictitious bill: Where both drawer and payee of a bill are fictitious persons, the acceptor is liable on the bill to a holder in due course. If the latter can show that the signature of the supposed drawer and the first indorser are in the same hand, for the bill being payable to the drawer's order the fictitious drawer must indorse the bill before he can negotiate it. (Section 42).

5. No effect of conditional delivery: Where negotiable instrument is delivered conditionally or for a special purpose and is negotiated to a holder in due course, a valid delivery of it is conclusively presumed and he acquired good title to it. (Section 46).

Example: A, the holder of a bill indorses it "B or order" for the express purpose that B may get it discounted. B does not do so and negotiates it to C, a holder in due course. D acquires a good title to the

bill and can sue all the parties on it.

6. No effect of absence of consideration or presence of an unlawful consideration: The plea of absence of or unlawful consideration is not available against the holder in due course. The party responsible will have to make payment (Section 58).

7. Estoppel against denying original validity of instrument: The plea of original invalidity of the instrument cannot be put forth, against the holder in due course by the drawer of a bill of exchange or cheque or by an acceptor for the honour of the drawer. But where the instrument is void on the face of it e.g. promissory note made payable to "bearer", even the holder in due course cannot recover the money.

Similarly, a minor cannot be prevented from taking the defence of minority. Also, there is no liability if the signatures are forged. (Section 120).

8. Estoppel against denying capacity of the payee to indorsee: No maker of promissory note and no acceptor of a bill of exchange payable to order shall, in a suit therein by a holder in due course, be permitted to resist the claim of the holder in due course on the plea that the payee had not the capacity to indorse the instrument on the date of the note as he was a minor or insane or that he had no legal existence (Section 121)

9. Estoppel against indorser to deny capacity of parties: An indorser of the bill by his endorsement guarantees that all previous endorsements are genuine and that all prior parties had capacity to enter into valid contracts. Therefore, he on a suit thereon by the subsequent holder cannot deny the signature or capacity to contract of any prior party to the instrument.

CHAPTER TWENTY-SEVEN

DISHONOUR OF A NEGOTIABLE INSTRUMENT

DISHONOUR OF A NEGOTIABLE INSTRUMENT :_When a negotiable instrument is dishonoured, the holder must give a notice of dishonour to all the previous parties in order to make them liable. A negotiable instrument can be dishonoured either by non acceptance or by non-payment. A cheque and a promissory note can only be dishonoured by non-payment but a bill of exchange can be dishonoured either by non-acceptance or by non-payment.

Dishonour by non-acceptance (Section 91)

A bill of exchange can be dishonoured by non-acceptance in the following ways:

1. If a bill is presented to the drawee for acceptance and he does not accept it within 48 hours from the time of presentment for acceptance. When there are several drawees even if one of them makes a default in acceptance, the bill is deemed to be dishonoured unless these several drawees are partners. Ordinarily when there are a number of drawees all of them must accept the same, but when the drawees are partners acceptance by one of them means acceptance by all.

2. When the drawee is a fictitious person or if he cannot be traced after reasonable search.

3. When the drawee is incompetent to contract, the bill is treated as dishonoured.

4. When a bill is accepted with a qualified acceptance, the holder may treat the bill of exchange having been dishonoured.

5. When the drawee has either become insolvent or is dead.

6. When presentment for acceptance is excused and the bill is not accepted. Where a drawee in case of need is named in a bill or in any indorsement thereon, the bill is not dishonoured until it has been dishonoured by such drawee.

Dishonour by non-payment (Section 92)

A bill after being accepted has got to be presented for payment on the date of its maturity. If the acceptor fails to make payment when it is due, the bill is dishonoured by non-payment. In the case of a promissory note if the maker fails to make payment on the due date the note is dishonoured by non-payment. A cheque is dishonoured by non-payment as soon as a banker refuses to pay.

An instrument is also dishonoured by non-payment when presentment for payment is excused and the instrument when overdue remains unpaid (Section 76).

Effect of dishonour: When a negotiable instrument is dishonoured either by non acceptance or by non-payment, the other parties thereto can be charged with liability. For example if the acceptor of a bill dishonours the bill, the holder may bring an action against the drawer and the indorsers. There is a duty cast upon the holder towards those whom he wants to make liable to give notice of dishonour to them.

Notice of dishonour: Notice of dishonour means the actual notification of the dishonour of the instrument by non-acceptance or by non-payment. When a negotiable instrument is refused acceptance or payment notice of such refusal must immediately be given to parties to whom the holder wishes to make liable. Failure to give notice of the dishonour by the holder would discharge all parties other than the maker or the acceptor (Section 93).

Notice by whom: Where a negotiable instrument is dishonoured either by non- acceptance or by non-payment, the holder of the instrument or some party to it who is liable thereon must give a notice of dishonour to all the prior parties whom he wants to make liable on the instrument (Section 93). The agent of any such party may also be given notice of dishonour. A notice given by a stranger is not valid. Each party receiving notice of dishonour must, in order to render any prior party liable give notice of dishonour to such party within a reasonable time after he has received it. (Section 95)

When an instrument is deposited with an agent for presentment and is dishonoured, he may either himself give notice to the parties liable on the instrument or he may give notice to his principal. If he gives notice to his principal, he must do so within the same time as if he were the holder. The principal, too, in his turn has the same time for giving notice as if the agent is an independent holder. (Section 96)

Notice to whom?

Notice of dishonour must be given to all parties to whom the holder seeks to make liable. No notice need be given to a maker, acceptor or drawee, who is the principal debtors (Section 93). Notice of dishonour may be given to an endorser. Notice of dishonour may be given to a duly authorized agent of the person to whom it is required to be given. In case of the death of such a person, it may be given to his legal representative. Where he has been declared insolvent the notice may be given to him or to his official assignee (Section 94). Where a party entitled to a notice of dishonour is dead, and notice is given to him in ignorance of his death, it is sufficient (Section 97).

Mode of notice: The notice of dishonour may be oral or written or partly oral and partly written. It may be sent by post. It may be in any form but it must inform the party to whom it is given either in express terms or by reasonable intendment that the instrument has been dishonoured and in what way it has been dishonoured and that the person served with the notice will be held liable thereon.

What is reasonable time?

It is not possible to lay down any hard and fast rule for determining what is reasonable time. In determining what is reasonable time, regard shall be had to the nature of the instrument, the usual course the dealings with respect to similar instrument, the distance between the parties and the nature of communication between them. In calculating reasonable time, public holidays shall be excluded (Section 105).

Section 106 lays down two different rules for determining reasonable time in connection with the notice of dishonour

(a) When the holder and the party to whom notice is due carry on business or live in different places,

(b) When the parties live or carry on business in the same place.

In the first case the notice of dishonour must be dispatched by the next post or on the day next after the day of dishonour. In the second case the notice of dishonour should reach its destination on the day next after dishonour.

Place of notice: The place of business or (in case such party has no place of business) at the residence of the party for whom it is intended, is the place where the notice is to given. If the person who is to give the notice does not know the address of the person to whom the notice is to be given, he must make reasonable efforts to find the latter's address. But if the party entitled to the notice cannot after due search be found, notice of dishonour is dispensed with.

Duties of the holder upon dishonour

(1) Notice of dishonour. When a promissory note, bill of exchange or cheque is dishonoured by non-acceptance or non-payment the holder must give notice of dishonour to all the parties to the instrument whom he seeks to make liable thereon. (Section 93)

(2) Noting and protesting. When a promissory note or bill of exchange has been dishonoured by non-acceptance or non-payment, the holder may cause such dishonour to be noted by a notary public upon the instrument or upon a paper attached thereto or partly upon each (Section 99). The holder may also within a reasonable time of the dishonour of the note or bill, get the instrument protested by notary public (Section 100).

(3) Suit for money: After the formality of noting and protesting is gone through, the holder may bring a suit against the parties liable for the recovery of the amount due on the instrument.

Instrument acquired after dishonour: The holder for value of a negotiable instrument as a rule is not affected by the defect of title in his transferor. But this rule is subject to two important exceptions

(i) When the holder acquires it after maturity and

(ii) When he acquires it with notice of dishonour.

The holder of a negotiable instrument who acquired it after dishonour, whether by non-acceptance or non-payment, with notice thereof, or after maturity, has only, as against the other parties, the rights thereon of his transfer. (Section 59).

CHAPTER TWENTY-EIGHT

NOTING AND PROTESTING

NOTING AND PROTESTING

When a negotiable instrument is dishonoured the holder may sue his prior parties i.e., the drawer and the indorsers after he has given a notice of dishonour to them. The holder may need an authentic evidence of the fact that a negotiable instrument has been dishonoured. When a cheque is dishonoured generally the bank who refuses payment returns back the cheque giving reasons in writing for the dishonour of the cheque. Sections 99 and 100 provide convenient methods of authenticating the fact of dishonour of a bill of exchange and a promissory note by means of 'noting' and 'protest'.

Noting

As soon as a bill of exchange or a promissory note is dishonoured, the holder can after giving the parties due notice of dishonour, sue the parties liable thereon. Section 99 provides a mode of authenticating the fact of the bill having been dishonoured. Such mode is by noting the instrument. Noting is a minute recorded by a notary public on the dishonoured instrument or on a paper attached to such instrument. When a bill is to be noted, the bill is taken to a notary public who represents it for acceptance or payment as the case may be and if the drawee or acceptor still refuses to accept or pay the bill, the bill is noted as stated above.

Noting should specify in the instrument,

(a) The fact of dishonour,

(b) The date of dishonour,

(c) The reason for such dishonour, if any

(d) The notary's charges,

(e) A reference to the notary's register and

(f) The notary's initials.

Noting should be made by the notary within a reasonable time after dishonour. Noting and protesting is not compulsory but foreign bills must be protested for dishonour when such protest is required by the law of the place where they are drawn. Cheques do not require noting and protesting. Noting by itself has no legal effect. Still it has some advantages. If noting is done within a reasonable time protest may be drawn later on. Noting without protest is sufficient to allow a bill to be accepted for honour.

Protest

Protest is a formal certificate of the notary public attesting the dishonour of the bill by non-acceptance or by non-payment. After noting, the next step for notary is to draw a certificate of protest, which is a formal declaration on the bill or a copy thereof. The chief advantage of protest is that the court on proof of the protest shall presume the fact of dishonour.

Besides the protest for non-acceptance and for non-payment the holder may protest the bill for better security. When the acceptor of a bill becomes insolvent or suspends payment before the date of maturity, or when he absconds the holder may protest it in order to obtain better security for the amount due. For this purpose the holder may employ a notary public to make the demand on the acceptor and if refused, protest may be made. Notice of protest may be given to prior parties. When promissory notes and bills of exchange are required to be protested, notice of protest must be given instead of notice of dishonour. (Section 102)

Inland bills may or may not be protested. But foreign bills must be protested for dishonour when such protest is required by the law of the place where they are drawn (Section 104). Here a bill is required to be protested under the Act within a specified time, it is sufficient if it is 'noted for protest' within such time.

The formal protest may be given at any time after the noting (Section 104A)

Contents of protest

Section 101 of the Act lays down the contents of a regular and perfect protest which are as follows:

1. The instrument itself or a literal transcript of the instrument; and of everything written or printed thereupon.

2. The name of the person for whom and against whom the instrument has been protested.

3. The fact of and reasons for dishonour i.e. a statement that payment or acceptance or better security, as the case may be, has been demanded of such person by the notary public from the person concerned and he refused to give it or did not answer or that he could not be found.

4. The time and place of demand and dishonour.

5. The signature of the notary public.

6. In the case of acceptance for honour or payment for honour the person by whom or for whom such acceptance or payment was offered and effected.

CHAPTER TWENTY-NINE

SUMMARY

A negotiable instrument is a piece of paper which entitles a person to a sum of money and which is transferable from one person to another by mere delivery or by endorsement and delivery. The characteristics of a negotiable instrument are easy negotiability, transferee gets good title, and transferee gets a right to sue in his own name and certain presumptions which apply to all negotiable instruments.

There are two types of negotiable instruments

(a) Recognized by statue: Promissory notes, Bill of exchange and cheques and

(b) Recognized by usage: Hundis, Bill of lading, Share warrant, Dividend warrant, Railway receipts, Delivery orders etc. The parties to bill of exchange are drawer, drawee, acceptor, payee, indorser, indorsee, holder, drawee in case of need and acceptor for honour. The parties to a promissory note are maker, payee, holder, indorser and indorsee while parties to cheque are drawer, drawee, payee, holder, indorser and indorsee.

Negotiation of an instrument is a process by which the ownership of the instrument is transferred by one person to another. There are two methods of negotiation: by mere delivery and by endorsement. In its literal sense, the term 'indorsement' means writing on an instrument but in its technical sense, under the Negotiable Instrument Act, it means the writing of a person's name on the face or back of a negotiable instrument or on a slip of paper annexed thereto, for the purpose of negotiation. A bill may be dishonoured by non-acceptance (since only bills require acceptance) or by non-payment, while a promissory note and cheque may be dishonoured by non-payment only. Noting means recording of the fact of dishonour by a notary public on the bill or paper or both partly. Protest is a formal notarial certificate attesting the dishonour of the bill.

The term 'discharge' in relation to negotiable instrument is used in two senses, viz.,

(a) Discharge of one or more parties from liability thereon, and

(b) Discharge of the instrument.

www.ingramcontent.com/pod-product-compliance
Ingram Content Group UK Ltd.
Pitfield, Milton Keynes, MK11 3LW, UK
UKHW021922190726
13853UKWH00002B/798

9 798888 495544